MY
BLUE
BLANKET

Choosing to Put It Away...

MY BLUE BLANKET

Joyce Landorf Heatherley

THOMAS NELSON PUBLISHERS
Nashville

Published in Nashville, Tennessee, by Thomas Nelson, Inc., and distributed in Canada by Lawson Falle, Ltd., Cambridge, Ontario.

Some Scripture quotations are from THE AMPLIFIED BIBLE: Old Testament. Copyright © 1962, 1964, by Zondervan Publishing House (used by permission).

Scripture quotations noted J. B. Phillips are from J. B. Phillips: THE NEW TESTAMENT IN MODERN ENGLISH, Revised Edition. Copyright © J. B. Phillips 1958, 1960, 1972. Used by permission of Macmillan Publishing Co., Inc.

Scripture quotations noted KJV are from the KING JAMES VERSION OF THE BIBLE.

Scripture quotations noted as NAS are from THE NEW AMERICAN STANDARD BIBLE, Copyright © 1960, 1962, 1963, 1968, 1971, 1972, 1973, 1975, 1977 by The Lockman Foundation and are used by permission.

Scripture quotations taken from The Holy Bible: NEW INTERNATIONAL VERSION are marked NIV. Copyright © 1978 by the New York International Bible Society. Used by permission of Zondervan Bible Publishers.

Scriptures quotations noted NKJV are from THE NEW KING JAMES VERSION. Copyright © 1979, 1980, 1982, Thomas Nelson, Inc., Publishers.

Scripture quotations noted RSV are from the REVISED STANDARD VERSION of the Bible. Copyright © 1946, 1952, 1971, 1973 by the Division of Christian Education of the National Council of the Churches of Christ in the U.S.A. Used by permission.

Scripture quotations noted LB are from *The Living Bible* (Wheaton, Illinois: Tyndale House Publishers, 1971) and are used by permission.

Library of Congress Cataloging-in-Publication Data

Heatherley, Joyce Landorf.
    My blue blanket / Joyce Landorf Heatherley.
      p.   cm.
    Includes bibliographical references.
    ISBN 0-8407-7599-7
    1. Self-actualization (Psychology)   2. Choice (Psychology)
   3. Attitude (Psychology)   4. Women—Religious life. I. Title.
BF637.S4H438   1991
248.4—dc20   91-27280
                                         CIP

Printed in the United States of America

1 2 3 4 5 6 7 96 95 94 93 92 91

In Memory of
My Father

Clifford Andrew Miller
1905-1987

CONTENTS

ONE

ONE LAST FREEDOM

Call it misplaced pride or an exaggerated sense of confidence, but after writing twenty or more books, I stayed home one day to start writing this newest one and, conceivably, to make my deadline with Thomas Nelson.

I even went so far as to announce with a slight flourish of arrogance, to all who would listen, that I wouldn't be in the office "for a while" as I was going to hole up at home to write *My Blue Blanket*.

So much for that delusional fantasy.

The mentally clobbering reality is that I came home, spent days setting out all my notes, chapter folders, and reference books. Finally, with all diligence and full steam ahead, I began writing into manuscript-form a talk I've been giving to audiences for over a year and a half. But after a few days of writing that same reality shouted, "Hey, Joyce, wait a minute. Virtually nothing cognizant has happened here. You have trashed each and every line so far, and you've several wastepaper baskets full of yellow lined paper to prove it!''

I saw my confidence and all its bubbling bravado evaporate faster than the steam from a boiling kettle of water. Leveled by this truth, I decided to put down my pen, leave the notes, books, and research papers on the dining room table where I was trying to work . . . and walk away.

"Go do something really important, like going out to the mailbox to bring in today's mail," I heard in my head.

So I did.

I leafed lackadaisically through the stack of letters and bills and ended up absentmindedly browsing through the newest edition of *Time*. I suppose I'd have gone on vaguely perusing its pages except that I came to the interview section and was stopped by the riveting, penetrating dark brown eyes of Mother Teresa staring up at me from her portrait at the bottom of the page. Not only did her eyes and face capture my attention but her gnarled hands spoke volumes to me. I wondered how many cups of cold water those hands had given in the name of Christ over the years in Calcutta, India.

Standing there looking at that page in *Time* magazine was one of those infrequent lightning-strikes moments. It was a second when you knew, you just knew, you should stand quite still, pay close attention, and remember the moment forever.

Then the heading about Mother Teresa's interview popped up and jumped off the page at me. It read, "A Pencil in the Hand of God."

I'll tell you, my unflinching self-assuredness flinched.

The title seemed to confirm my worst-case-scenario feelings about my own writings. Without a second's delay, I slid down an emotionally greased slide and fell into a swirl of dusty self-doubts and a pit filled with the gravel of my insecurities. No matter how stalwart, how fearless or how confident I am when I sign a book contract, to actually write a manuscript is quite another thing.

"A Pencil in the Hand of God"?

For crying out loud, I thought. *Any writer, Christian or not, would most certainly kill (or pay a high-priced publicist) to be called a writer who is a "pencil in the hand of God"!*

My second flash of insightful rhetoric was almost as dull as the first one, but perhaps a tad more realistic. I began to give free rein to my imagination as to how good I would feel if some journalist, Christian or not, were to write that Joyce was a pencil in the hand of God.

Of course, my serious reading of the interview revealed that the title did not generate from the pen of Mr. Desmond, the journalist, but had come from Mother Teresa herself. And it had come in an answer to an incredulous Mr. Desmond asking—I can see his raised, questioning eyebrows—*"You* feel you have no special qualities?"

Mother Teresa responded without an ounce of self-aggrandizement, without a trace of hypocrisy or poor-me attitude, and definitely without hiding behind the mask of pseudohumility. "I don't think so," she said simply and then continued, "I don't claim anything of the work. It is his work. I am like a little pencil in his hand. That is all. He does the thinking. He does the writing. The pencil has nothing to do with it. The pencil has only to be allowed to be used. In human terms, the success of our work should not have happened, no?"[1]

Eagerly I read on, not because I see myself as some

glorious, 24-carat gold pencil in the hand of God but because I never see myself as a pencil at all. But that's beside the point. (Forgive the pun.)

The real issue here is not the pencil, its size or even the prolific volume of words the pencil produces. It's who's holding the pencil, and in this case, it's the hand of God.

I write with a Paper Mate™ pen, but I picked up a pencil from the pen tray before me and studied it.

The pencil alone is a rather useless item. It can't think. Can't love. Can't begin to communicate. Can't cry. Can't feel anguish or outrage or speak for itself. But let someone pick up this ordinary yellow, eraser-headed pencil and push it against a surface, and it becomes almost alive, a viable tool capable of pouring out an absolute torrent of thoughts, ideas, and concepts, even dreams. The pencil becomes an instrument which brings meaning and purpose to the pure joy of being here on this earth as a child of God.

Reading the interview with Mother Teresa was a wonderful glimpse into the soul of this extraordinarily rare, beautiful, and committed woman of God, a woman who, in this day and age when skepticism runs deep, especially as it relates to religion in general and God's children of all religions in particular, responded to the journalist's questions with a shimmering mix of King Solomon's wisdom and an innocent little girl's naiveté.

Near the end of the interview, her remarks touched my heart with an authenticity and reality that was most refreshing, and in a way, I find this hard to describe.

It seems to me that the older I get, the more I see God continually working through many other people, like Mother Teresa, and how often he uses their words or

[God] works through others, even if I do not agree with them or they with me.

their deeds to speak so clearly to me. He does this even when I am not of their particular religious persuasion, and something else: He works through others even if I do not agree with them or they with me.

I'm ashamed that I had to be this old before coming around to such an obvious fact about the way God works. Apparently, others like Dr. Robert A. Cook, wiser than I, saw it some years ago for he expressed it well when he wrote: "I remind you: God reserves the right to use people with whom you and I may not agree. Oh yes. He does!" And later he stated, "Methods are never sacred. It is the gospel that matters."[2]

Here I am a dyed-in-the-wool gentile protestant Christian woman, born with a father who was an independent and evangelical minister and a mother who taught and lived the Bible her whole life. Yet God surprises my heart every once in a while as he did today while I was reading the article which quoted Mother Teresa. It's as if God took his own pencil and erased our differences, at least for a brief shining moment, and whispered, "Open up your eyes, your ears, and your soul because here's something I want you to think about. Here's something I want you to absorb and learn."

Mother Teresa and I are quite literally worlds apart— she in Calcutta, India, and I in Austin, Texas. Then, too, there's that little matter that I've never been a nun in a Catholic order and I know very little of her personal lifestyle, her joys or her aching heart. She has never married or been divorced. Yet we are both children of God.

As I read on in the interview, I was unprepared for the journalist's pointed, almost intrusive remark. He said, "There has been some criticism of the very severe regimen under which you and your sisters live." I was equally unprepared for Mother Teresa's concise answer: "We choose that."

I found myself deeply moved, and somewhere in the depths of my soul, Jesus' words "Take up thy cross and follow me" were garden-fresh.

Perhaps there is never a day, an hour, or even a moment when in some way we do not make a choice of some kind. From our first moments of wakeful thinking and deciding to get up or stay in bed after the alarm has rung, to the millions of tiny, insignificant events or the large momentous crises which thunder in on us like rolling storm clouds, down to the last occurrence before sleep mercifully grants us a short adjournment . . . there are choices to be made.

The word *choice* is by no means new to any of us; in fact, I think, given the mind-set of our present society, we have overworked the word so much that it has become commonplace and jaded. And precisely because it is so often used in book titles, bantered about in conversations, and strewed around in various dialogues, we tend to accept the myth that surrounds the act of choosing. It has become easy to minimize its enormous significance and complexity. After all, we reason, to make a choice is an uncomplicated, simplistic, effortless thing. We imply that any addled featherhead can easily make a decision.

Even my dictionary adds to the absurdity of the issue by saying that choice is merely "the act of choosing . . . selecting from two or more things that which is preferred."

It's simple, see. You just choose. Right? Wrong! Perhaps no word in our vocabulary presents more obstacles to our thinking than the word *choice*.

Great importance was given to this word by the internationally renowned psychiatrist Dr. Viktor E. Frankl. As I reread his insightful comments about choices, I began to assimilate the immense complexity of choosing and the desperate need of choice to cope with the joys as well as the sufferings of our lives.

Dr. Frankl's book *Man's Search For Meaning* was written after he was freed from years as the prisoner Number 119,104 in Auschwitz concentration camp. In his book he tells of questioning himself while he was still incarcerated in the death camp. He talks about human liberty and spiritual freedom and ultimately asks, "Does man have no choice of action in the face of such circumstances?"[3]

Dr. Frankl assures us as he goes on to write, "We can answer these questions from experiences as well as on principal. The experiences of camp life show that a man does have a choice of action. Man can preserve a vestige of spiritual freedom, of independence of mind, even in such terrible conditions of psychic and physical stress."[4]

But I find myself coming back time and time again to Dr. Frankl's powerful statement about the choices we can make and his introduction of another word: *attitude*.

Hear the heart of this great man as he wrote of Auschwitz:

We who lived in concentration camps can remember the men who walked through the huts comforting others, giving away their last piece of bread. They may have been few in number but they offer sufficient proof that everything can be taken from a man but one thing: the last of human freedoms—to choose one's attitude in any given set of circumstances, to choose one's own way.

Fundamentally, therefore, any man can, even under such circumstances decide what shall become of him —mentally and spiritually. He may retain his human dignity even in a concentration camp. . . . It is this spiritual freedom—which cannot be taken away—that makes life meaningful and purposeful.[5]

How profound. Here is a man who was stripped of everything he held dear and was left naked, as it were, to live out his days. Mother, father, brother, and beloved wife had all perished in the death camps. Only one sister survived; yet, he tells us that not only do we have the freedom to choose but we also have the freedom to choose what exactly our attitude will be toward others and toward the circumstances of our lives.

The moment we choose, as my dictionary puts it, our preference of one thing over another is a moment in our lives far from being uneventful. No, it's a very difficult and highly disciplined maneuver, and if we grasp the immense value of choosing our attitude, I believe we will have caught on to one of the most powerful truths of our lives.

Dr. Frankl's emotional and spiritual sanity was preserved by his choice of attitude. Observing him, one cannot help but stand in awe of the human ability and power of choice—not that choice of attitude is ever easy.

Even when prisoner Number 119,104, in his pathetic "boots" made of scraps of leather and held together with bits of wire, was being marched along the winter-frozen roads to the work sites around the concentration camp and forced along by the guards' rifle butts, he was still able to choose his attitude. He found a refuge from the terrifying emptiness, the icy temperatures, the appalling desolation and spiritual poverty by choosing the attitude of his thoughts.

Dr. Frankl's method was to talk mentally to his wife on those hideous walks, never knowing whether she was alive or not, but always imagining her answers to him. He said of his thoughts during those gruesome journeys, "Nothing could touch the strength of my love, my thoughts and the image of my beloved."[6]

Apparently what makes a choice a not-so-easy accomplishment is when we add attitude to it. Yet, however it is with our attitude, so goes our whole life.

Perhaps you're thinking, "Oh come on, Joyce. Attitudes affect our whole world?"

Yes, precisely. Attitudes are of paramount importance in our lives for they influence our mental state, hence our frame of mind. They shape and form our mind's outlook, its tendencies, and lay the foundation for our biases, our opinions, and our prejudices, and therefore, ultimately, our choices and actions.

I'm sure, at one time or another, you've worked or lived with someone whose attitudes shaped his or her thinking into a particular mind-set. His or her mind-set could be anything from a deeply critical and negative one to a sunshine-bright, affirming and positive one. But such people's ability to affect or modify our own attitude can be downright surprising. Just think of the enormous power attitudes hold over our emotions and responses to others. In fact, attitudes are so powerful that sometimes they are stronger than the actual words we speak.

After I'd finished a speaking engagement not too long ago, I was signing books, hugging people and being hugged, when a delightful woman stood before me. By the look on her face, I knew she never expected to meet me this side of heaven. In an almost awestricken voice, she said, "Oh, I saw your film series years ago, but I want you to know you are much more beautiful now than you were then."

My self-confidence shot up some thirty degrees as I knew the film series was shot in 1981 and in what feels like minutes I'm going to be a shot sixty years old.

Then, while I was still tap dancing on the table of my emotions, the woman added, "Of course, you've put on a little weight since then, but you're still more beautiful now."

Of course, I've put on a little weight?

For about a half a second there I wanted to be offended, but I couldn't be. Her face and her tone of voice reflected such a great and loving inner spirit and attitude that all I could do was laugh, agree with her, and repeat her line to my husband, Francis.

Patting my hips, I said something like, "Yep. I'm beginning to look more like my Hungarian mother and grandmother every day."

I realized that someone else could have said those same words to me, but with a critical or negative attitude, and my feelings would have been crushed. This woman's loving spirit and affirming attitude spoke far more eloquently than her words, and my heart responded to that attitude rather than to what she said.

Attitudes can do anything from transforming our feelings and our responses in heart-stirring, touching ways to the other extreme of creating piercing pain. The attitudes of others and ourselves can harden or melt our emotions any hour or day of the week.

As attitudes influence us mentally and emotionally, their impact spills over and shows up in our body language. A poor attitude or an attitude of low self-esteem, for instance, can easily be identified in our demeanor, our walk, our posture, and yes, conspicuously in our general appearance or more noticeably on our faces.

A doctor once told me he could check patients' progress by whatever their attitudes were concerning their appearance. When hospitalized patients perceived they were getting well, their attitude shifted from depression and an apathetic indifference about their appearance to a hopeful concern about looking their best—men wanting to be shaved or have their hair combed and women wishing aloud their hair could be washed and wanting a touch of lipstick.

Attitudes do give visual messages, good or bad, positive or negative, to those around us.

So when we understand the significant role attitudes play mentally, emotionally, and physically, there seems to me, no way one can ignore the magnitude of the need to choose the best attitudes for our lives. I believe that long after we are gone, we will be best remembered not so much for what we've accomplished as for what our spirit, the essence of our attitude, has said and left behind. It is our attitude, the real spirit of our soul, that will continue and remain for others to remember.

Mother Teresa's answer in the *Time* interview about her own choice to live in a "severe regime" reflects an

impressive attitude. Both she and Dr. Frankl deliberately
used their human freedom, choosing their attitudes, and
it spiritually freed them to have, as Frankl would put it,
an enormously "meaningful and purposeful" life in
spite of death, poverty, or hideous circumstances.

---

*It is our attitude, the real spirit of
our soul, that will continue on and
remain for others to remember.*

Forgive me if I sound like I'm obsessed with the idea
of choosing our attitude. Perhaps I am. But when one
has lost everything and is daily living in the bowels of hell
like Frankl was, I want to know how he did it. How did he
go from victim to survivor? And did he merely survive or
did he move into recovery? There it is in every reading:
he claimed "the last of human freedoms—to choose
one's attitude."

Then when I read David's words, "Where is the man
who fears the Lord? God will teach him how to choose
the best" (Ps. 25:12 LB), I have to believe that God is in
this with me, helping me to "choose" what is best for
me. I can trust him not only for my salvation but for my
peace of mind as well. David goes on to say,

> *My eyes are ever looking to the Lord for help, for he alone
> can rescue me. Come, Lord, and show me your mercy, for I
> am helpless, overwhelmed, in deep distress; my problems go
> from bad to worse. Oh, save me from them all! See my
> sorrows; feel my pain; forgive my sins. See how many ene-
> mies I have and how viciously they hate me! Save me from*

them! Deliver my life from their power! Oh, let it never be said that I trusted you in vain! Assign me Godliness and Integrity as my bodyguards, for I expect you to protect me and to ransom Israel from all her troubles.

(Ps. 25:15–22 LB)

David chose to have the attitude of trust in spite of the despicable circumstances and the enemy all around him. Perhaps it was the attitude of trusting God that carried him through the sin and the shattering events of his existence. Strike *perhaps;* I know it was David's choice of attitude that made him "a man after God's own heart."

Two sisters who lived in New Testament times and had a difference of opinion regarding attitudes were Martha and Mary. Jesus talked about Martha's attitude of over-reacting and fretting about getting things done and Mary's attitude of quiet reflection at the master's feet. Their lives point so clearly to the fact that we do choose our attitudes.

Moses' attitude, as recorded in Hebrews 11, tells about the choice he made: "It was by faith that Moses, when he grew up, refused to be treated as the grandson of the king, but chose to share ill-treatment with God's people instead of enjoying the fleeting pleasures of sin" (Heb. 11:24, 25 LB).

But I suppose the most convincing illustration from scripture would be in Philippians 2:1–5. Here the apostle Paul is telling the people in Philippi how to get along and work with each other but, more importantly, I believe he gave them a key to understanding how to keep their personal relationships well nourished. In the fifth verse he tells them a secret: "Your attitude should be the kind that was shown us by Jesus Christ" (LB). Or as J. B.

Phillips's translation reads, "Let Christ Jesus be your example as to what your attitude should be."

And since attitude is a choice as well as a mind-set, see this same verse in the good old King James, "Let this mind be in you, which was also in Christ Jesus."

For some time now I've been turning over in my mind the truth about the amazing difference my attitude (positive, negative, or indifferent) makes in my life. I've also become keenly aware of the high-tech degree of difficulty of finding practical, down-to-earth ways of choosing the attitudes that God would have me, as his child, fashion into the weaving loom of my life's tapestry.

I'm not a theologian having gleaned my training and knowledge in the classroom of some highly accredited seminary, but I am, as I said, a child of God. And since our Lord makes a very big point of emphasizing our need to have open, receptive minds and to have honest and truthful emotions as a child does, then I must start to find those practical ways of choosing attitudes, trusting childlike, that God will teach me "how to choose the best."

I must start to find those practical ways of choosing attitudes, trusting childlike, that God will teach me "how to choose the best."

TWO

I CHOOSE TO GIVE UP MY GLITTERING IMAGE

I have always cared about my image, or more to the point, I have always cared what other people *think* about my image. Why it has been of such all-fired importance to me is absurd, I agree. But I figure you and I (well, maybe not you, but certainly I) started this obsession with caring about others' opinions very early in our lives.

Throughout my childhood and into my adult life, I know that I've gone to great lengths to appear to other people as wonderful, talented, intellectual, gracious, wise, generous, and considerate. Why? So that you and others will like me. As I look back on it now, being liked by others seems always to have been very high on my emotional agenda.

When my children were little, I hated imposing restrictions on them because I wanted them to like me. Later, in their teen years, I was constantly trying to find ways to be with them, to help keep the communication channels open, and to give them good memories of their growing-up years because I wanted them to like me.

Today, when I'm with my children or speaking with them on the phone, I just want to express my love and my beliefs in their abilities because I am still back at wanting them to like me. I won't even go into the ridiculous lengths I try to have my grandchildren like me, as I'm sure you get the picture.

I can't abide the thought of ever appearing anything but warm and wonderful. Certainly I want no one to describe my personality or my character as awful, cold, untalented, stupid, foolish, stingy, or cruel. No, not me. I want everybody to see my fantasy of perfection, my this-is-the-way-I-really-am look. I want you all to love the shimmering me, to approve of the sparkling, effervescent me, and to think I'm, in a word or two, splendidly bright. Why? Again, so you will like me.

On the other side of the coin, I wish I didn't care quite so much! I'm also tempted to wish my attitude was a little more like Lucy's in Charles Schulz's *Peanuts* cartoon.

Somewhere along the way, Lucy and the delightful old lady named Flora, whom I described in *The Inheritance* (Austin, TX: Balcony), passed the point of caring or worrying if they were liked or not. They have reached the place in life and time where they don't care or think about impressing others with their greatness, talent, or goodness, nor do they seem to care in the least what others may say or think about them. They have somehow stripped and sanded themselves down to their real, un-varnished true selves, saying what they think and letting the chips fall where they may.

In the *Peanuts* cartoon I have before me, the meek and gentle Charlie Brown looks incredulously at the insup-pressible Lucy and seeing that her mouth is zippered into a tight, straight line across her face, he says as point-edly as he dares, "I see you're wearing your crabby face again today."

Lucy whirls around to him and spits out, "There's nothing wrong with being crabby." She adds in the next square, "I'm proud of being crabby." Then, in the last square of the cartoon, Charlie is standing in place like a bronzed statue, and Lucy, not caring what anybody, in-cluding Charlie—especially Charlie—thinks of her and not worrying in the slightest about her image, lets Char-lie have the *Real Lucy*. I love it!

She combines body language (her right arm topped by her closed fist is raised defiantly over her head) with her soul language (she bellows defiantly at the top of her lungs) to Charlie and the whole world, "The crabby little girls of today are the crabby old women of tomorrow!"[1]

What a picture! Wouldn't you like to care less and have more of Lucy's brassy veracity? But alas, I'm not Lucy, or Flora for that matter. And I care plenty about what others think of me. I've always cared!

It's precisely because I do care so much that I go to great lengths to present a public image that will please you, that will justify my actions or my responses. That, as they say in business, is the bottom line: to help you to like me!

Caring what others think of me started early in my life, as I'm assuming it did in yours. I cared first about what my parents, especially my mother, thought of me. I saw to it that my image was spangled, tinseled, and sequined, even when I was very young. I knew that when my mother said in front of company at home or congregations at church, "Joyce-Honey, sing the new song I taught you," I was to sing. I would do whatever she asked because if I did, everyone would like me. Even at three years of age, my outer image began developing, especially when I sang.

At age six and seven, piano lessons began, and then elocution lessons were added. I pounded the piano keys, memorized and recited many poems, readings, and monologues. At eight, I began the years of singing, acting, and general performing in school plays and musicals, which continued all through my educational sojourn, even into college. At ten, I accompanied my father on the piano when he sang, as well as the children my mother conducted in her youth choirs and the congregational song services at church. I also sang solos and played the Autoharp™. By the time I was eleven, I composed my first song and accompanied myself as I sang it for my junior high's spring musical. By age twelve, I placed first in the vocal competition for the state of Michigan.

At age thirteen, my plan to get people to like me was given a stunning blow. It happened in my P.E. class.

I discovered rather quickly that as long as I was the lead in every school play or was asked to perform at every given opportunity, my "fantastic" image shone and seemed to encourage others to like me. Best of all it seemed to please everybody, especially my parents and the people at church. But my gym class was a horse (a whole herd actually) of a different color.

I found my much admired, even envied, performing image could not be depended upon to get me through gym class. I was devastated every Monday, Wednesday, and Friday, convinced that I was everything I didn't want to be. Having my sparkling "self" pulled away left the plain ole' me for everyone to see and evaluate. And it was devastating!

I thought it was that glittering, performing image that made others, especially my peers at school, like me. But down inside, I feared that if people who admired my talents ever saw the real me, or if they were to take a good look behind the glitter, beyond my ability to sing, play, act, or perform, well, I just "knew" the real Joyce would leave much to be desired, in fact, a whole lot to be desired. And the result? Ah, ha! They wouldn't like me at all.

I felt then what psychologists have since called shame. But at the time I couldn't have defined it that way.

As I've stated before in other books, it seemed as if I was always ill when I was a child. Much of the time, I was sick with the usual, and three times the unusual, childhood diseases and malaise. When I was ten years old, I had four months of rheumatic fever. So from then on in school, instead of taking physical education classes like everyone else, I was assigned *Rest*.

Why the students in Rest, who spent the class time "resting" on a cot, were required to suit up in shorts, blouses, and tennis shoes and—I could never understand this—take a shower at the end of gym with everyone else, only God and the P.E. teachers knew.

Even if you didn't have Rest instead of gym class, I'll bet (though I'm not a betting lady) you can vividly recall the first time you undressed and, dying of self-consciousness, showered with thirty-five other girls. Never mind that all thirty-five were as naked as jaybirds just as you were. The experience probably made an indelible and humiliating impression on your soul. It sure did on mine.

The first thing I learned was that the horror of taking showers, which had a great deal in common with the ancient Chinese water-drip torture or the persuasive stretching rack of medieval times, was inflicted first, foremost, and unmercifully to two specific types of girls in the shower room: them that had very big ones and them like me, who had none at all.

I learned much later that this notorious humiliation was not limited or confined to my gym classes. It was practiced and refined on a grand scale in most every girls' shower room in every school, in every country, and has continued through several generations.

Since I was this skinny girl who had absolutely no emboosiasm whatsoever and was cement-slab flat . . . I grew intensely protective and sympathetic to a fat girl named Doris, who could barely stand up straight because she was so top heavy with a glorious abundance of mammary glands. We both were singled out every Monday, Wednesday, and Friday. If we accidentally stood together in the shower room, all the cheerleader-type girls, those with the I-would-kill-for figures and their perfect, not too big, not too small, just right B and C cup bras, let Doris and me have it with their stream of hysterically funny observations and comparisons. We stayed in a constant state of mortification. We also stayed as far apart as possible in the shower room.

---

*. . . the early scarring of our souls
. . . can and does doggedly pursue
and follow each of us. Those old
derogatory remarks can hang on in
our minds.*

Of course, now, in the light of nuclear war, homelessness, poverty-stricken people, and terminal diseases, I can look back on those gym classes I dreaded so terribly and realize that having no emboosiasm was no big deal. I can even laugh with you now as we look back and share our similarly humiliating experiences. Since I am a little more grown up now, I know that the belittling put-downs, which once so annihilated my self-worth, are just that—put-downs—and a part of the painful puberty process.

Still, the early scarring of our souls, which can happen routinely during those puberty years, can and does doggedly pursue and follow each of us. Those old derogatory remarks can hang on in our minds. At least, for me they did and led me to believe sincerely, even after I was an adult, that my body and particularly my lack of breasts were, at the worst, something to be ashamed of and at the least a joke.

Then, in my mid-forties, after those years of conditioning which convinced me that I was ugly, I was stunned with a surprise development. (Pardon the pun.) Out of the blue I became, as they say, a late bloomer. And wonder of wonders, I developed emboosiasm in a rather pleasing way!

Many women have asked about the cure for cement-slab flat, whispering, "What did you do? Was it secret creams? Push–ups? Workouts or what?" I don't honestly know, unless perhaps it was all those years of praying and begging for at least a small portion of something to help my blouses and dresses to hang better on me.

I find it mildly amusing, the way we act as if we are not hurt by the negative evaluations of others. We keep up the smiling; yet, inside of us a completely different scenario is going on. At the same time my own public image (by then I was speaking and singing all over the world) looked very glamorous to others, my own private perception of myself was vastly different. Yet, I doubt anyone guessed. Funny. The early scarring of my emotions in the gym showers carried over all those years, and I might never have seen my real true self or worked through the early scarring except for an experience that helped me to reevaluate my public and private images.

Not many months after I'd had my fiftieth birthday, I was at a church in Florida speaking at a women's conference. Somehow, as I was talking to the 800 or more women, I gestured with my hand to emphasize a point. At almost the same time, I twisted my body slightly, flung out a short little kick with my leg, and almost passed out with the pain. Later, it was ascertained that I'd pulled a whole bunch of tendons. It took weeks to heal.

During the excruciatingly painful part of my recovery, my daughter Laurie and my then two-year-old grandson, James, came out to my home to take care of me.

The first morning I was able to get out of bed, a very apprehensive Laurie slowly and carefully led me to the bathroom to take a shower. Gently, she helped me out of my nightgown.

But instead of helping me over the step into the shower stall when I was ready, Laurie stood there and stared at me. Finally, after a few moments, I waved my fingers which asked, "Hello, anyone at home?"

Ignoring my remark and looking at my bare breasts with obvious admiration, Laurie really shocked me. "Mom," she asked, "do I have to be fifty years old before I have beautiful breasts like yours?"

I thought her question was most preposterous and quite silly. Quickly, I explained, "Laurie-Honey, I don't have 'beautiful' breasts. What do you mean?" My mind was already repeating the negative comments I'd heard over the years, and even though I'd seen the obvious changes in my figure, I was still believing that nothing about my body was beautiful or even vaguely nice.

"What do *you* mean?" Laurie countered. "You don't think you have beautiful breasts?" Her look questioned my mental abilities. Gently but determinedly, Laurie turned me around to face the big mirror above the double sinks.

"Look," she gestured toward my reflection. "They are beautiful!"

Coming from the teasing and belittling of the gym class shower and locker rooms to years of being self-conscious about my appearance, I stood there realizing I'd never heard in my whole life the word *beautiful* used to describe any part of my body, much less those parts.

How does it happen, I wondered, *that we often have a reasonably well-put-together image for others to see yet inside, where it counts, we are really languishing in loneliness and filled with a contemptuous type of self-shame? Do other people, like me,* I asked myself, *appear to be sparkling and beautifully put together on the outside, glowing with success, yet have an inner awareness about the dull, grimy film of loneliness spreading through them? Do they sense the ever tarnishing process going on in their soul, which continually blackens and eventually ruins their self-esteem?*

Merikay, a co-worker with us at Balcony Publishing, shoved a thick paperback novel in my hands not too long ago and breathlessly gushed, "Joyce, you've got to read this. It's great! It's about a bishop in the Church of England and is set in the 1920s. You'll love it!" I'm reasonably certain that neither of us then had any idea how profound an influence it would have on my life.

I looked down at Susan Howatch's novel. The white raised letters of the title, *Glittering Images,* stood out dramatically against a shocking pink foil background and I thought, *Glittering Images? What does that mean and why is Merikay so insistent not only that I read it but that I'll love it?*

Of course, by page four, I was committed.

Glittering Images is the first book in a series of novels about bishops, archbishops, and monks and their human nature in the Church of England, in the early twentieth century. An emotion-packed story about God, people, and Church leadership, it involves a wonderful tale of godly counseling, forgiveness, and the healing that comes to a person when under fire from a series of painful events and unwanted dire circumstances.

The story line shows bishop and widower Charles Ashworth being forced to admit and study the fact that he sees something about himself he has never seen before: He has two distinctive images.

Charles Ashworth's archbishop asks him to spy on another bishop and arranges for him to spend a few days at the palatial home of the bishop in question. Charles settles into the bishop's guest room and then decides to go for a drive in the country. He takes off his "clergyman's uniform" and puts on some casual clothes.

Charles's moment of truth about himself breaks in upon him as he surveys his image in a long glass mirror, deciding and then deciding not to wear a tie. Fiddling with the top button of his shirt, he makes the silent observation that he looks pretty much like what he is: an off-duty clergyman. Then, for some unknown reason, he takes a closer look at the mirror and explains:

> But then I looked in the glass and saw the spy beyond the clergyman, the image beyond the image and beyond the spy was yet another man, the image beyond the image beyond the image. Reality blurred; fantasy and truth became inextricably intertwined. I told myself I had imagined the distant stranger but as I felt my personality begin to divide I covered my face with my hands.
>
> Sinking to my knees by the bed, I whispered: "Lord, forgive me my sins. Deliver me from evil. Help me serve you as well as I can." After that I felt calmer, and when I glanced again in the glass I found that the off-duty clergyman was now the only visible image.[2]

I won't spoil the plot for you because the bishop's quest to unravel the intricate meanings of his "image beyond the image beyond the image" is a fascinating tale. What he learns in those few moments as he is looking into the mirror follows him throughout the whole book. His seeing the image beyond the image set my heart to racing, though, because I've always suspected a truth about myself and perhaps about all of us. But I've never read or heard anybody describe the phenomenon in such graphic terms: admitting, in kind honesty, that when we look into a mirror, it is possible to see our two images. Call it what you will, I think it's more than highly possible for us to have two distinctive images within our beings.

From the first pages of this ingenious web of events and emotions until I finished it, I barely laid the book aside. Then, I clearly understood why Merikay had thought this novel about England's clergy would intrigue me.

As I read the novel, every once in a while, I'd hear little popping noises in my mind, and I knew it was the sound of puzzle pieces snapping into place. I'd briefly stop my reading to catch my breath and, with wide-eyed wonder, say aloud to myself, "Oh yes, that's me. I've been right there. So that's why I did so and so or felt such and such or reacted and responded in that particular way!"

My glittering image is my public persona. It's perhaps the only me you'll ever see.

Like the Bishop Charles Ashworth, we have one very visible image: the one we'd like others to see, admire, and respect—our glittering image. The other image (behind the image) is not really an image at all but our true self. We rarely see our true selves, much less let anyone else observe closely. Instead, it lies hidden beneath and behind our glittering outer image.

After I finished the novel, I mentally looked into my own "long glass" and carefully studied my reflection. I, too, saw the image beyond my image. I've gone to elaborate lengths to keep it polished, sparkling, and untarnished. Let me describe it for you.

My glittering image is my public persona. It's perhaps the only me you'll ever see. It's my image when I'm with you at your home, the office, marketplace, church, or in public anywhere. It is the image I want and dearly wish you to see, to like, to respect, and to admire.

My glittering image shimmers as it masks my pain, anger, resentments, even the abuses in my life or anything else I wish to keep hidden.

My glittering, sparkling image is my disguise, my camouflage, my pretense that fairly shines and exudes, "Hey, everything is under control. I'm strong, self-sufficient, just fine. I'm okay, even if my relationships in my marriage or my family are not just ailing but are very sick, perhaps in the throes of dying or dead already."

My glittering, bedazzling image, my body language, and my verbal soul language blind you and shield me from letting you know what I really think or feel.

As I peered closer in my mental mirror, I tried deciphering the second, shadowy, and elusive image behind the glittering image: my true self. My task grew much more complicated. I'm far more familiar with that public persona of mine than with the true self I keep hidden in the privacy of my soul. Here's a description of my true self.

My true self is my private persona. It's the me you may never see.

My true self is my unvarnished self that bears the burden, the blame, and the responsibility of my difficult past and my frantic present.

My true, bare, naked self is my yearning self, hungering for mercy and grace both from God and mankind.

My true self is my authentic self, haunted by the ghost of fearful memories and new information that bring dark, menacing shadows over what I already know.

My true, unembellished self is one that battles with false and needless guilt and with guilt that's earned the old-fashioned way, by sin or regrets, which seeks and needs forgiveness.

My true, bare, naked self is my yearning self, hungering for mercy and grace both from God and mankind.

My true, genuine self is not as bold and fearlessly courageous as I'd want you to believe but is often timid, confused, deeply frustrated and, at times, estranged and isolated from the rest of the world.

My true, natural, unadorned self is consumed with the effort and perpetual sense of struggling to carry out the details of my life's mission.

J. B. Phillips wrote of the differences between quality and quantity in the introduction to his book *Good News*. He explained that "quantity can be impressive":

Now although most of us are wide awake to the difference between quantity and quality in things, I don't think we are nearly so sensible in our judgment about people. We're far more impressed than we ought to be by the quantity of a man's gifts and sometimes we are slow to appreciate the quality or lack of it in his life. For instance, it's only too easy to be dazzled by a man who's a clever talker, possesses that indefinable something that we call "charm", has plenty of drive, is good at games and is what is called a "good mixer", and never see that he has all his goods in the shop window. We may fail to see that the real quality of his life is poor and shallow. And indeed, as long as he gets away with it, the poor chap may not see it himself.[3]

(Funny how we seem to go for glittering image quantity every time.)

But Phillips continued:

The ordinary current judgments of the world are very often based on a man's outward possessions. People say, "He's worth so many thousands" or "He owns so many thousand acres," or "He's written a bestseller" or "He's very popular on the radio," and treat the man with respect and admiration in consequence. In fact, the quality of the man's life may be very poor, spiritually; he may have little or no knowledge of God, and no spiritual resources to draw on if things go wrong for him. Jesus rightly insists that what really matters is quality. What sort of person are you? In the eyes of God—that is, in Reality for that is always what matters.[4]

As I read these remarks by J. B. Phillips, I began to see between the lines the relevance of the glittering image and the true self to his description of the quantity and quality of life and character. The impressive quantity of our gifts, or our public persona, that Phillips talked about is our glittering image and the quality of the life we actually live is our true self. He enlarged on this thought when he added:

> Now suppose you were to ask yourself in all honesty this simple question: "What sort of a person am I?" I don't mean, "What do I possess?", and I don't mean, "What have I achieved?" and I certainly don't mean, "What sort of impression have I made on other people?" But I do mean, "What am I in the eyes of God— what sort of quality do I possess in my inward life?"[5]

It is possible to change a few things on our own to be more "true-self" and more inner-quality directed people. We can learn to discipline ourselves (a hard lesson for some of us—talk to any author about the discipline of writing or to a student about the discipline of studying).

Phillips talked of our choice in becoming people of quality and penned a line I love:

> We have the ability to choose [ah, there's that word] whether our lives are completely self-centered, or whether they are really given to the best interests of our fellowmen. Up to a point, then, we can do something, and if we have been lucky enough to have had a sensible Christian upbringing there will be quite a lot of good things that we do almost automatically. Yet I am certain that for most people, if there is to be any real and lasting change of quality of living, they need someone outside themselves to help them. The direction of our lives, and therefore their quality, will depend on what in our heart of hearts we love, and on what in our heart of hearts we really believe.[6]

J. B. Phillips gave us grace when he said that we can *choose quality* on our own, but he warned us about the reality that on our own we will run out of ideals, become discouraged, and give up. So what we need—and I believe this with all my "heart of hearts"—is to choose to get in touch, as he said, with "God focused in the person of Christ." In him we'll find the highest possible *quality* of living. And as we "transfer our faith from ourselves to him . . . we begin to understand God, his purpose and our part in that purpose."[7] Then, we can truly begin to see the worth of our God-given true self and, at least gradually, give up the unnecessary baggage our *glittering* image is forcing our true self to carry.

In my own world today I know I have this choice before me: I can choose outward quantity of life or inner quality of life. If I go for the glittering image, I may bedazzle a great many of you, including myself. But if I go for the true self with a lot of help from the Lord, each step I take will make the difference. Then, I can choose to give my life a higher quality, a meaningful quality, a purposeful quality, and a quality that will outlast my earthly existence by a long shot.

Now, if I'm so smart and have figured out this much, I have to ask myself . . . why is it so hard to push beyond my glittering images? Why can I not just consistently or routinely focus in on being my true self? Why do I think it so important not only to polish my glittering image but to cling dearly to it? Why don't I quit hiding behind the polished splendor of what I want you to see and get real . . . open up and let you and the world around me see my true image . . . my very truest inner self?

Part of the answer lies in the fact that there's a familiar comfort and ease in doing what we've always done—in this case, hiding in the shadows of our glittering image. And many of us truly believe that our real self is the sum total of what we've accomplished or how much we possess or what gifts we have . . . when, in fact, those things do not determine the inner quality of our true, real self.

It's unreal, even unnatural, to our psyches to think about emerging and setting one big toe out from behind that safe place and allowing our true self to be seen in broad daylight. I must face the fact that no matter how dedicated I am to getting rid of my hypocritical and phony glittering image, I am scared about just being me and exposing my true self.

There are also a number of times in life when discarding the glittering image and paring down to the true self might be not only unwise but extremely painful to me and possibly destructive to someone else.

Maybe these thoughts have occurred to you and you're way ahead of me.

You may recall that during those vulnerable early years of your life, you did emotionally lay aside your glittering image. You took out your true self and put it on the table for someone or for all to see, as I did physically when I stripped down for the gym class showers. But it took only one heartbeat for you to figure out and understand that after you risked allowing your real self to be shown, two things, two dreadful things happened. One scenario involved you and the well–being of your emotions, and the other scenario involved someone else and the well–being of their emotions.

Perhaps during those early years of your life when you were less worldly wise and far more trusting than you are now, you courageously stepped out from behind your well-formulated glittering image and honestly became your true self, only to be amazed that what others perceived and heard from you seemed to be completely different from what you had intended or meant. You were horrified when some people grossly misunderstood the motives and the meanings of your true self. Others were sincerely offended, and some did not take your true self seriously or, worse, did not believe you at all! At times the words you used when you were being your true self were turned and used against you. I've learned these things in the very hardest of ways.

At best, it's risky business to step out from behind our glittering image, but for me it was particularly harrowing because of my successes as a Christian woman, wife, mother, musician, speaker, and author.

My marriage to Francis Heatherley signaled the end to what little I had left in regard to former friendships with others.

That rejection of friends and certainly of Christian leadership because of my divorce and remarriage was and is strong and crushing. Hindsight and research of the word *rejection* has taught me that rejection, whether real or merely imagined, in any relationship is one of life's most difficult and unpleasant experiences. And dealing with nagging rejection saps one's strength and energy at the core level. The controversy and stigma of my choices concerning divorce and remarriage constantly rose before me like the great wall of China.

I'll never forget going to a large charity event. Though we personally knew a great many of the people who attended, we spent the entire evening with three or four people speaking only very briefly with us and the rest of that huge throng looking past, through, or around us. It was a weird experience to go almost overnight from a highly visible person to an invisible human being.

Two years after that depressing experience, some Christian couples, on the spur of the moment, invited us out to a social gathering. Because invitations were exceedingly rare, we were thrilled at the idea of being with this peer group. There were authors, publishers, and clergymen. Just to be invited out felt *wonderful.* However, that "great time" of being together quickly eroded into something else.

The couples asked how things were going with us in the aftermath of divorce and remarriage. I decided to play it straight—no glib, glittering-image answers, no responding with what I thought they might want to hear. Instead, I would answer just as matter of fact as I could, tell-it-like-it-is-from-my-true-self-Joyce.

Big mistake.

Hardly anyone cared or wanted me to be my true self. One of the men, on hearing some of the details, gave a short lecture entitled, "You made your bed, now you lie in it." Another suggested we forget all that stuff and "move on with life." (Whatever that means.)

It took only a very few minutes of wading into the pond of true self to realize that the friends we were with were merely making conversation and didn't actually want to hear anything negative or real—just the good and glorious reports. The pond turned into quicksand. These peers weren't interested in hearing about the massive rejection we were feeling or the fallout of acid rain pouring down around us, nor were they interested in the slightest about our recovery process.

After hearing me describe some of the pain Francis and I had been going through, the author seated next to me, who was also a pastor's wife, looked directly at me as if I were either certifiably demented, suffering hallucinations, emotionally unsound, or just pulling her leg and loudly proclaimed, "Oh, I don't believe it!"

To not be believed after you've poured out your heart, whether it's to a friend, a counselor, a pastor, or a physician, always comes as a shocking surprise and devastates one to the core. When the woman repeated a third time, "Oh, I don't believe it!" I ran as fast as my little legs could carry me, right out of that true-self quicksand back into the safety of my phony "Everything's just hunky-dory" glittering image.

When I stopped answering the questions with my true-self answers and gently slid behind my glittering image, my "Oh, I don't believe it!" woman settled into what can only be described as a "comfort-zone" conversation with me. She detailed the events of her day, which were about her fabulous shopping spree in the mall.

I'm sure she and the others were relieved with my silence for that seemed to excuse everyone from dealing with us, our pain, or the hard and complex but true facts of our life.

Perhaps you can recall a time when you bared your true self to someone and wished you'd cut off your tongue first. I can.

I've had a number of times, especially in the past six years, when I shared my true self with someone I trusted. I told a friend and several Christian counselors and pastors my most intimate feelings and thoughts, only to discover later they had repeated what I told them.

We are devastated when our confidence is broken. Friendships or counseling therapy can be destroyed forever. The searing humiliation of betrayal after we've been so vulnerable in revealing our true self lowers our "trust-for-others" factor significantly. Finding the grace to forgive and trust those individuals again becomes a very difficult and formidable task. It's hard to carry on with our journey because we can be heavily handicapped by bitterness, which is a close companion of broken confidences.

The second problem with baring ourselves and showing our true self, as I've said, is what our true self verbally can do to others. I have had the experience of, inadvertently and without malice of forethought, giving a terrible blow to someone by saying something from my true self. I have watched in horror as my true self has either annihilated someone's personhood or come dangerously close to doing so. I don't want to hurt myself or, God forbid, someone else, but crassly blurting out my true self may not be in my or anyone's best interest.

I am a wife, mother, grandmother, mother-in-law, and now, for the first time in my life, stepmother. This latter role I'm cast in is wonderful and awful at the same instant.

Relationships between stepparents and stepchildren tend to be fragile at best, and the adjustment time to the new relationship varies with each individual. I know that, at times, I've wanted to be my true self and say exactly what I thought was highly appropriate, maybe even needed, but I also knew it was not the right thing to do. Instead, I choked back the words and left them unsaid because no matter how noble or good my intentions were, to say what my true self was thinking might have leveled one of my stepchildren's personhood.

It seems when another person's emotional safety is at stake, I should be prudent and step behind my glittering image, at least for the time being. But is hiding the right way?

Even with these various pitfalls in being my true self, I must find a way to break out, to push beyond the false glittering image of mine if I am to have the rich quality of life I crave.

In the past few weeks, I've been dealing with the opportunity of choice I have about my images, especially in regard to relationships, and I find I must choose my attitude very carefully.

I'm sure you can see the dilemma here. There are problems in both the glittering image and the true self, so at times we must come up with an attitude that delicately stands somewhere between the dangerous hypocrisy of a glittering image and the equally dangerous, cruel, and crass exposure of the true self. I can't simply choose to discard my glittering image, even though it represents a rather false me, and go through life just being my natural, unadorned true self, baring and blaring my intensity of feelings from within.

So the thought occurs to me that rather than walking around my world, covered and concealed by my outrageous glittering image costume . . . perhaps the answer lies in my needing to clothe my true self. I don't mean I need to clothe my true self with a dazzling sequined costume designed to hide my faults, my failures, or my sins and make me look glamorously perfect. But rather, sometimes, instead of showing to the world only my naked true self, I need to clothe myself in the gossamer silk garments of kindness, patience, understanding, forgiveness, and most of all, grace, not only for others but for myself as well.

Years ago, my mother gave me this delightful clipping:

ONE OF THESE DAYS I MUST GO SHOPPING

I am completely out of self–respect and self–esteem. Since I'm a child of the King I really shouldn't act so impoverished.

I want to exchange that self-righteous skirt I picked up the other day in Sunday school for some simple humility they say is less expensive and wears better over the years.

I need to look for some tolerance and patience which are being shown as coats and wraps for the fall season.

Someone showed me some beautiful samples of peace . . . I seem to be running low on that and one can never have too much of it!

Also, before I forget,

I should go to the alterations lady and have my sense of humor dress mended . . . it's torn in several places. And perhaps I can look for some inexpensive everyday goodness while I'm at it.

I might go to that specialty shop and try on that little undergarment of long–suffering that they are displaying in their window. I really never thought I wanted to wear it . . . but I feel myself coming to it.

Oh yes, and by the way,

I must try to match some grace that my neighbor wears so often. It is so becoming on her and I think the color of grace might look equally well on me.

It's surprising how quickly one's stock of goods is depleted.

Yes, I must go shopping soon.

—Author Unknown

This kind of clothing on my true self can help to serve as a buffer in the war zone of our relationships with people.

Clothing our true self with kindness can protect innocent people, including ourselves, from pain. Clothing our true self with grace can provide a safe place where sometimes we wisely reserve the right to withhold some or all of the truth of the information within our minds because it would wound and bring pain to others. Clothing our true self with understanding can help us to remember that it might not be prudent or in anyone's best interest to confide to others our opinions, feelings, judgments, or choices. Clothing our true self with patience gives ourselves and others a second chance, another try, perhaps even a measure of hope.

We clothe ourselves, not out of deceptive motives at all . . . but rather because of other factors . . . like poor timing or knowing that information would destroy our or someone else's personhood or consideration for someone's pain. In short, I believe in the need for clothing our true self out of consideration for the protection and well–being, and yes, even comfort of ourselves and others.

The other night, as Francis and I were discussing the difficulties with both a glittering image and our true self, we began talking about this need to protect the true self within all of us. Quite suddenly, he began giving me an analogy about cars. I almost tuned him out because cars are not at the top of my priority list of interesting things to discuss. (Unless, of course, he is going to talk about getting me a car of my own, namely a white Mazda convertible.) However, even though I'm not "into cars," I found his analogy a good description of the need and the wisdom of clothing our true self for protection and comfort.

A car, Francis pointed out, does not need a body complete with a roof, sides, windshields, or upholstered seats to get us from one place to another. All a vehicle of any kind needs in order to be used for transportation is a frame and engine, wheels, steering and gear mechanisms, and fuel. That stripped-down "frame-with-engine" car is the true self.

For protection against the elements, and for the comfort of the driver and passengers, we need a body to cover the bare frame. We need the sides, the roof, and the windshield. Inside, we have the padded seats, the heater and air conditioner, even the radio to insulate, protect, or give us comfort. Adding those parts of the car is like adding the clothing of grace to our true self.

To take this one step further, it can be said that even a car has its own glittering image.

For eleven years I drove a Mercedes 450 S.L. All I really knew about it was that if I put the key in the ignition, it would transport me where I wanted to go. Still, I was not oblivious, unaware, or untouched by the admiring stares and flattering comments people always made when I was driving that pretty powder blue 450 S.L. It was my glittering image car.

Francis and I have sold the car and have been a one-car family for a couple of years. But when I see a 450 S.L. on the highway, I feel a slight twinge of nostalgia. I liked the glitter.

We now own an Oldsmobile station wagon, which is somewhere between the glittering image Mercedes and a true-self-stripped-down-to-the-bare-chassis car. It transports us safely, serves us well, especially when we are hauling books or display baskets for Balcony Publishing, and is very comfortable. It's our true-self car with clothing.

Does any of this make sense to you? I hope so. I'm trying to make the point for myself and for you that we do have a choice about what we allow others to see when they look at us: the glittering image which hides everything or the true self which, at times, is clothed with grace.

Unfortunately, as I said before, it is not an uncomplicated or easy thing for any of us to break away from or push beyond our glittering image. I usually protect my glittering image, even when I most sincerely desire to shed it in favor of my true self, particularly with what I say. Whether we like it or not, our speech betrays us in many ways. Glittering images are seen first . . . true self later.

To the world around us, we children of God are far more famous for our hypocrisy than our faith.

We talk in spiritual circles and clichés, especially when we are with our pastor or other church leaders. We foolishly hope they will be impressed with our polished glittering image. We also hope that others will be impressed by the glittering spectacle of what we say. After all, we want them to "like me."

We quote scriptures to validate our religious image. We try to impress others by commenting on our dedication to prayer. Yet, for all our pious talk about how holy our habits are and how we don't use the Lord's name in vain, we may drink wine in secret with other Christians who also, in secret, drink wine. And sometimes when things are going from bad to worse in our lives, we feel the freedom to describe our lives by a four-letter word——, confident and safe, knowing they'll protect our glittering image language as we protect theirs.

The truth is, we Christians want to be freed from this, but it won't happen until we face this and say it out loud.

Once in a while, our lack of speech, in fact, our silence betrays us and our glittering image. We clam up and get real quiet when we know we should be speaking up on someone else's behalf. We're afraid of saying something that would spoil or detract from our own sparkling glittering image, so we protect it by being silent.

Sadly, at times, we take verbal, emotional, even spiritual abuse from other Christians about our faith, or lack of it, for we don't want anybody to think we've got a problem with God, his silence, or his "No" answers to our prayers. Our glittering image takes over our true selves and dances to the tune of "everything-is-just-fine-thank-you."

Right along with protecting and polishing our glittering image there is an extremely dangerous myth which raises its dragonlike head when we least expect it.

It's the myth that says we as Christians don't have a glittering image. The myth spins out the rationale that because we are free in Christ, we never hide behind our glittering image but live out our lives as our true selves clothed in grace. Not only do we go into denial about the existence of a glittering image but we do terrible things and play awful games in disguising that true self of ours.

I say this is a dangerous myth because in my years of being involved in church circles (remember, I was born with a minister father and a Bible–teaching mother), I've seen how destructive we children of God can be in denying we have a glittering image.

I don't know about you, nor is this chapter written to

come down hard on any of us, our glittering image or our true self. But for me, my glittering image (and I do have one!) needs to crack and peel off my soul, wither and die. And with God's help, I can choose to make that happen. In fact, no one but me can peel off my glittering image. I am the only one who can do anything about it.

I have the extraordinary freedom to choose my attitude, but as long as I hide, retreat or go into denial behind my glittering image, it will rule me, it will control me, it will make my choices for me. I can't let that continue to happen. It's not my true self or what I believe God had in mind for me as his child.

So the big question is, If I do choose to strip away my glittering image, how in the world do I go about it? I don't want to live behind a glittering image or distort my true self, living as a phony Christian woman—the world has enough examples of Christian hypocrisy. But I've become so good at protecting and preserving my glittering image and at times I fail to clothe my true self with grace: So I wonder . . . where do I start?

In the novel *Glittering Images,* when Bishop Ashworth sees his "image beyond the image beyond the image" in the long mirror, he responds first—before he knows how these images will affect him and before he seeks help from a monk in a monastery—by sinking to his knees and whispering an urgent prayer. He asks the Lord to do three things: "Forgive me my sins. Deliver me from evil. Help me serve you as well as I can."

A great but basic prayer there. And though it is a secular novel, the author is right on target with the priorities of the prayer in the proper order if the bishop is to begin breaking away from his *glittering* image.

This was the moment when the bishop decided against living for the glittering *quantity* and began to give serious attention to the *quality* of his life. The process really does have to start with our relationship to God.

There is absolutely nothing we can do to force God to like us.

It is important to start this prayer to God by asking him to forgive our sins, even if we feel that we have no big sins, only little "white-lie" sins. Someone said, "We are all sinners except on different subjects." It is no fluke that letting go of our glittering images usually begins with initially admitting our sins on a daily basis, asking forgiveness from God, then, moving on to receiving protection from God, and finally, enlisting help from God.

There is no more positive beginning toward healing and recovery than when we begin by petitioning God through prayer. But there's more good news.

When we come before the Lord in our glittering image, there is absolutely nothing we can do to force God to like us. He sees right through our glittering image, and no matter how it shines, our glittering image is utterly useless before him. We have no ability, no power, and no persuasive talents that could possibly impress or cajole God into liking and approving of us. Nor can our glittering image, no matter how dazzling, blind God from seeing and knowing our true self. God looks through and past that phony glittering mask and always sees us, our real person, our true self. After all, it was God who made the true self.

God is not the inventor of the glittering images we all wear so defensively. Rather, the opposite, he made us in his image and started us out on quite a different path.

God inspired the writers of the scriptures to describe the true self, not the glittering images, of every character. He could have allowed us to see only a parade of cover-up masks and glittering images of his people, but he chose not to do this. He chose to portray his people, starting with Adam and Eve, and going through Noah, Abraham and Sarah, Isaac, Moses and David, *as they really were*. By the time we get to the New Testament with Jesus, his disciples, and the people of those times, we have to realize that if God wanted us to see the glittering images of his people, he'd have written a lot more razzle-dazzle into the script and left out a whole lot of true-self pain and anguish.

Nothing is hidden from God. When I realize and remember this and I seek his face and forgiveness, his unending mercy and his unfailing grace, I can rush to God without my ever–present glittering image. I am free just to be my true self. I can feel the joy and the freedom from his unconditional love. The thought that God is not impressed with my glittering image, that he sees my true self and that he loves me anyway (or in spite of me) moves me to the depths of my heart and stirs a fire of love in me toward him.

So the first place we begin the peeling off of our glittering image is before God because he knows and understands the desires of our heart—namely, that we want to be our true self—and as I've said many times, because we can trust God to see our true self. I do believe we can trust God when he says, "I take great delight in you." He truly is our heavenly Father and unlike some earthly fathers he is not shocked, surprised, disappointed, or even impatient with us. He recognizes and sees beyond the glittering image to the true self of all his children, always, as God explained to Jeremiah, "to save [us] and deliver [us]" (Jer. 15:20 RSV).

There is a brief scene in George MacDonald's novel *The Gentlewoman's Choice* that persists in coming to mind as I write of our need to know God loves us, cares for us, and protects us, despite the condition of our true self—strong or weak, courageous or fearful.

The novel is about a Christian family, the Raymounts, who lived in England during the reign of Queen Victoria. A cousin of the family, a retired army major, decides to help out the family by spending time with one of their children, Mark, a frail and ailing boy of ten. A rich relationship develops between the boy and the major, who is continually amazed by Mark's simplicity of faith and warm friendship with God.

In this particular scene, the major sits by Mark's bedside telling story after story about his army days when he fought in India for Queen Victoria:

> One day he was telling the boy how he had been out alone on a desolate hill all night; how he heard the beasts roaring round him, and not one of them came near him. "Did you see him?" asked Mark.
>
> "See who, Sonny?" returned the major.
>
> "The one between you and them," answered Mark, his tone subdued. And from his tone the major understood.

"No," he replied; and taking into his the spirit of the child, went on. "I don't think anyone sees him nowadays."

"Isn't it a pity?" said Mark. "I wish God would call me. I know he calls some children, for he said, 'Samuel, Samuel.' "

"What would you say?" asked the major.

"I would say, 'Here I am, God! What is it?' We mustn't keep God waiting, you know!"[8]

The lines that haunt me as I write today are Mark's: "Did you see him?" And when asked who, his answer comes: "The one *between* you and them."

When we look into the long glass mirror, we can understand why we cling to our glittering images so tightly. There, in the dark shadows all around us, are the beasts no one but us can see—the beasts of loneliness, failure, depression, and hopelessness. No wonder we are afraid to let go of our shining glittering images.

We need to look at the whole mirror . . . to see the *One* who stands between us and them. We need to see him, the one who is here, the one between us and all those dark things that threaten us. We need to remind ourselves, as I'm sure George MacDonald did when writing his novel, of John 14:19, which says, "Yet a little while, and the world seeth me no more; but ye see me: because I live, ye shall live also" (KJV). We need to see the Lord standing between our true self and the beast stalking around out there in the dark—waiting to devour us. We need to see the one who knows and loves that true self of ours, yes, even the child within us, no matter how damaged, broken, or frail that child is. Oh, how desperately we need to entrust our true self to our heavenly Father and to see "the one who stands between us and them."

When I see that *One* standing between those beasts and me and realize that God really is on our side, I find it a little easier to peel away my glittering image. I find it a little simpler to break away from caring so intently about what others will think of me or hoping so much that others will like me. It's even possible that if I see my true self as God sees me and "delight" in that, I will begin to like myself a little bit more. And wouldn't that be a switch for most of us?

I find a significant measure of hope in knowing I can trust God and in choosing to be my true self, especially when I clothe that true self in grace. Because my glittering image cannot impress God into liking me, I find freedom from the hypocritical chains and bondage of my glittering images when I choose to risk being my real true self and ask for the forgiveness that's needed for God's deliverance and protection from evil and for his powerful help as I try to serve him.

I choose this attitude of life—being vulnerable and seeking forgiveness—as difficult as it is sometimes, because I'm dreadfully weary of polishing and protecting my glittering image. I'm sick of hoping that everybody from God to you will like me. Oh, I still want you to like me, but my very existence on this planet does not need to be controlled by my wanting everyone's approval or needing it for my own self-esteem.

I'm ready, past ready actually, to be my unsequined, untinseled true self. What I'm not ready to do is go about life, blatantly tossing out "cruel honesty" remarks, regardless of who they may hurt, all in the name of doing my own thing, being real, or letting others see my true self. No, that's not in anyone's best interests, certainly not mine, and it's not what I want at all. Rather, I'm ready to lay aside my glittering image. I'm ready to choose to be my true self clothed in grace for both you and me.

I sincerely believe that when we Christians venture forth into the risky business of being real, discovering daily who we are as God's children, and praying for God's forgiveness, protection, and help, our true self will serve God, ourselves, and humanity infinitely better than a lifetime of our glittering image would. I also believe that the quality of our lives will have more meaning, more purpose, and more direction.

It's our choice, yours and mine.

THREE

I CHOOSE TO ACCEPT MY HURTS

In a hotel, just hours after a United States federal court acquitted her on all counts, Imelda Marcos, the former first lady of the Philippines, granted an in-depth television interview.

I might have missed it as I rarely watch daytime television. Even now, I can't recall why, on this particular afternoon, I was flipping past the channels; but suddenly on my TV screen, there was a full head shot of Mrs. Marcos. She was saying, "It is just awesome. . . ." Her tone was quiet, almost muted, and her manner somewhat somber; yet, she commanded my undivided attention, riveting me to the screen.

She went on, "It is so . . . to be found not guilty on all counts was like . . . like being born again." Her facial expression was serene and touched with a trace of wonder as if she were describing a miraculous and mysterious out-of-the-body encounter. She seemed unable to take it all in.

Intently, I watched. As I've said many times, I'm vitally interested in anyone who has gone through an unbelievable *unworld* event. I want to know how they felt, what they said, what kept them going, how they responded to suffering, what they learned, what gave them hope, and mostly, who were those rare balcony people who affirmed them? Who was the friend who, as a small plaque hanging on my wall describes, is "one who walks in when the rest of the world walks out"?

Hastily, I grabbed my pen and tablet of paper to scribble down the interview. Mrs. Marcos was explaining quietly, "You know that for four years I was deprived of everything. I was deprived of my home, my country, even my beloved husband, my family, my personal items . . . everything. I felt skinless . . . just skinless . . . and everything hurt."

Then, at this point, I felt the woman conducting the interview seemed to go on the offensive, hostile side. I listened as the reporter began to minimize Mrs. Marcos's pain by saying in a cold, impersonal voice, "But we know you had many close friends in high places . . . powerful friends. You didn't lose them."

Mrs. Marcos looked away briefly before answering.

"Yes, I had important friends—that's true, but . . ." her voice trailed off and again she looked away.

"I mean," the interviewer persisted, "your close friends were big-name, important women like Nancy Reagan and Barbara Bush . . . people like that who were there for you." Again the statement seemed framed as a put-down to her grief and losses. Silence hung between the two women.

Mrs. Marcos settled back into her chair slightly. I sensed the struggle going on within her over the delicate issue of how to admit the truth without damaging herself or others in the process.

Finally, after more hesitation and a deep breath, Mrs. Marcos said carefully, "Oh yes, I do have powerful friends. . . . I think, though, they are very busy women with a great deal on their minds."

The interviewer was not about to move off the point. After another uncomfortable silence, Mrs. Marcos directly ascertained with wisdom born out of experience, "When you are deep in crisis, it is not the big or the powerful people who come to you," she paused and her face softened as she continued. "It's the ordinary, the little people, not the big, who come to be with you. Little people come and support you."

How true, I thought. In the six years since my separation, divorce, and remarriage, it was hardly ever the big, important friends who came to me, who wrote or called me. It was ordinary people, "little" people who were there for me and who supported Francis and me with their love.

Mrs. Marcos's commentary shot through the TV like an arrow sent straight to its target and found its mark in my soul, dead center. I could understand her relief at being acquitted, and I could well imagine her feeling "skinless" because of the raw scraping of my own soul. But I could also identify with her "sadder-but-wiser" feelings about the disappointments one finds in human nature. To me, the quintessence of the interview was the pain and brokenness (no matter how it came about) of simply being alive on this planet.

At this moment I can hear some of you saying, "Imelda Marcos? What do I have in common with her?" I understand. The odds of you or I being the first lady of even a small country are zip and none. However, the odds of our hurting and suffering to similar depths of an Imelda Marcos are a sure thing—set, as it were, in concrete.

You and I and the majority of people alive and living in this world . . . will at some time suffer.

Oh certainly, you and I may have stretches in our life span where we experience relatively little pain. (I can remember one six-week period, when I was seven years old, back a hundred years ago, when I was pain free and for once, no teacher had sent me to the principal's office for a "talk.") Maybe you can recall the months or the years when pain seemed to leave you alone and it took a vacation from you and your family. No one died or had a major illness. No one divorced; no one declared he or she was gay or filed for bankruptcy. Your kids gave you a break. They behaved well with others and even obeyed you. During this same time frame you may have suffered a slight concussion, some minor scrapes and bruises, and a few "green stick" fractured bones, but you simply took it in your stride and moved right along.

But let me put this down into words. You and I and the majority of people alive and living in this world—Christian or not, rich or poor, famous or failures, housed or homeless, well fed or starving, healthy or ill, whole or broken—will at some time suffer. None of us can escape the problems and the pain of being hurt.

I don't intend to be a voice of doom. I am wiser and older in life experiences than that. I know about that blessed hope of ours in Christ Jesus. I possess that mysterious and satisfying peace the world simply cannot understand. I rejoice and praise God for all his forgiving love, his endless stream of kindness, mercy, and grace.

But at the same time wisdom and age give us this kind of knowledge, they also give us a different perspective and help us to identify the epidemic of hellish pain exploding in our own life and in the lives of countless people everywhere.

Rather than going to one extreme of denying the fact that pain is happening or to the other extreme of dwelling and wallowing in it endlessly, for my own sake (and possibly yours), I want to set down a few examples starting with what I've gleaned from my personal tryst with heart-crushing pain and what I have heard you say about yours.

I know, for example, what Imelda Marcos means when in great awe she talked of being acquitted on all counts and likened it to being "born again." Can't you feel her relief? Don't you remember the joy of your own acquittal by God? I do. I recall the heaviness of spirit as I lugged my sins over the threshold and crawled into God's room called "grace." I remember not only the pain of my sins but the extraordinary relief and joyous celebration of God's merciful forgiveness.

I understand Mrs. Marcos's word *skinless* as I'm sure you do. We've all had a time when our skin was pulled and peeled away by scathing, even pious, criticism and we were "deprived" of people and things we held dear. Some of us are skinless now. We cannot stand being hugged, especially by the person who skinned us. We can identify with Mrs. Marcos's gentle grief over the silence and the loss of "big, powerful friends," but at the same time we can feel her wonder over the "little people" who came instead.

Some of us are skinless now. We cannot stand being hugged, especially by the person who skinned us.

Many of you are my longtime readers. You know better than anyone, about your own pain, but you also know a great deal of the pain I've chronicled in more than twenty books. You know of the grief losses which have left their monstrous footprints across my soul. You know that pain concentrated itself into intense emotional suffering beginning when I was thirty-two years old. Within that year and a few months, I experienced the death of my infant son, David, the death of the only grandfather I'd ever known and loved, Peter Uzon, and the death of Marion Uzon Miller, my dearest friend and fifty-seven-year-old mother.

Pain assiduously followed those grief losses. For eleven years, I suffered excruciating and devastating levels of physical pain because of a TMJ disorder, a dysfunction in the jaw joint. The disorder generated huge levels of head and back pain. During this same time, emotional pain began its harassment as I was trying to hold what was left of my marriage together.

Pain finally delivered another blow when after thirty-two years of marriage, there was an agonizing separation, followed a year later by an *unworld* divorce.

Pain was, by now, just getting warmed up. In the six years after the divorce and my new marriage, other sorrows seemed to come out of nowhere, striking from behind with shattering new information. The pain of lost-forever relationships, rejection and invisibility, watching others trying to discredit my life's work, has annihilated my self-esteem and will to go on. So pain continues to try to clobber the very life out of my being.

But still, I am alive. I am surviving and learning beautiful things about that *room called Grace.*

However, when we are at this hard place, we are sorely tempted to believe that no one in the whole world knows how we feel because no one in the world has faced the exact set of torturous circumstances we have. But we have to know that, though it's true my particular circumstances, my pain levels, my grief losses, my sins, my crises, and my vicissitudes will differ significantly from yours, we err when we tell ourselves no one understands or can possibly identify with or relate to us.

Sheldon Vanauken wrote of this feeling of aloneness we all experience when we suffer in "An Afterword" in his novel *A Severe Mercy.*

It is, I think, that we are all so alone in what lies deepest in our souls, so unable to find the words and perhaps the courage to speak with unlocked hearts, that we do not know at all that it is the same with others.[1]

The real truth is . . . it is the same with others. We are not alone. We are especially not alone in our suffering or sorrow.

Other people—millions, in fact—like you and me are invisibly bonded by hurt. Pain has penetrated each and every crevice and hollow space in others just as it has in us. We have become, for a thousand different reasons, people of pain. And some of us, because of the nature or circumstances of that pain are as untouchable as the lepers in Jesus' day.

We have become, for a thousand different reasons, people of pain.

We people of pain have begun to learn the lessons of pain. We have documented the fact that life can stab, sting, smash, bite, bruise, whip, and pommel us within an inch of taking our life. We people of pain are left with our minds and emotions maimed, scarred and sometimes paralyzed for life. Maybe to some of you who have not yet endured severe pain, or who are temporarily in a remission from pain, these words have been overly dramatic and you are like the pastor's wife who kept saying to me, "Oh, I don't believe it."

Of course, reality pounds home its message; and

whether others believe us or not, we do suffer. We people of pain belong to a huge multitude (yes, a majority) of people all around us who sit by the side of life's road, dazed and stunned, wondering where we are, who we are, and what has slammed into us.

Here is a small sampling from the phone calls, letters, and personal encounters I've had in recent weeks. They are real people like us who are on a first–name basis with pain. Here are some of the current events which are propelling them deep into the fires of pain. Their stories are true. I've not made them up out of my fertile imagination, but I have withheld their names and some of the details to protect them and others from anymore pain.

The woman who . . .

has undergone one scathing attack after another from other Christians on her work and her mission in life. She feels her whole life is being dismantled and discredited. She is facing the pain of forced oblivion as well as other points of suffering and humiliation. Over the phone she told me how she wanted to give up and she talked of taking her life. "It hurts all over and I feel skinless." She talked about her feeling of being without hope or joy and the feeling of her own worthlessness. She talked and we talked but, oh, dear God, can she endure much more pain without losing her mind or taking her life?

The woman who . . .

is a twenty-nine-year-old single parent to five children. She believed the "self-proclaimed prophets" who came to visit her from her church. First, they said she should not have divorced her former husband but should remarry him. Then, after she did remarry her husband, he, as abusive as ever, left her pregnant and about to give birth to twins. These same people said "God told them" that he would either save her former husband so she could remarry him again or God would kill him so she'd be free to marry someone else! She wrote to me:

> Because I believed they were closer to the Lord than I was—I believed them. I also believed I would not survive, and within weeks I was a mess. All hope was gone. I had a six year old, a two and a half year old, a fourteen month old and nine week old twins. I was drowning, and everywhere I turned there were Christians throwing more water in my face. Jesus is the only reason I am alive to write this letter. The hand of God kept the gun away from my head.

I'm glad to report that God is still bringing this courageous young single mother through, but I've shared a part of her painful life to illustrate the fact that there is an abundance of broken, hurting single parents all around us; and though our own pain may not be of the exact nature of the women I'm listing here . . . pain is pain. The Bible clearly tells us that when one member of the body suffers, we all do. Perhaps your pain and hurt lie in a different direction.

Maybe you are like . . .

The woman who . . .

is afflicted with a steadily deteriorating, life-threatening disease, like systemic lupus, a disease from which our precious friend Connie Parker suffered unimaginable degrees of pain.

Connie began corresponding with us when I moved to Texas in 1985. Francis and I fell in love with her wise-beyond-her-years-spirit and her soft and gentle voice. Even as we loved her, we loathed her lupus and what it did to her physically and emotionally. But nothing daunted Connie's spirit, and in our letters I never knew exactly who it was that did the ministering or who ministered to whom the most.

Sometimes we talked her through a night of pain by long distance phone calls to her home. But more often, she'd call or write us at just the very moment when our raw wounds needed the oil of her soothing words.

One of her cards in 1988 told us that lupus was getting the upper hand:

> Things have been unbelievable. Hold me tight in your mind and maybe I'll feel it.
>
> I've been in the hospital a lot—they let me come home for a couple of days to rest and hug my kids. Please pray—the pain—oh, the pain.
>
> I'm thinking of you all the time, praying for you and loving you!

Four months later God did relieve Connie's pain and she, just thirty-four years old, went home to be with him. We still miss her. We shall until we see her again.

The many women who . . .

though now in their thirties or older, are in great need of therapy and professional counseling because of the physical abuse or incest inflicted on them when they were little girls. They have suffered hideous assaults on their bodies, minds, and emotions. Some women, like the ones I'm remembering now, have endured abuse by men, a father, stepfather, grandfather, uncles, cousins, male family friends or neighbors. However, as unreal as this sounds, I'm hearing a new nightmare unfold as many abused women talk to me at my speaking engagements and write in their correspondence. It is a fact that an alarming number of women have experienced their trauma of sexual abuse and incest not from men but from other women: a mother, grandmother, aunt, cousin, niece, and occasionally an adoptive mother or stepmother.

If you are a victim of any sexual abuse, then you may know too well that even though the damage was done years ago or has been buried deep within you for years, a seemingly innocent incident can occur, and in the flash of a second the repressed memory shoots to the surface of your mind in a post trauma flashback, tearing anew at the old scars inside you. Once more, you are ripped open and hemorrhaging. That thing, that horrible thing, you realize, has never left you but has lain in wait inside and has grown up with you. It has followed you into every age. It is there now, eating away silently at the viscera of your life.

If you are such a woman, you will identify with books like Jan Franks's *A Door of Hope* (San Bernardino, CA: Here's Life, 1987) and Dan Allendar's *The Wounded Heart* (Colorado Springs: Nar Press, 1990). But most of all you are dearly relieved that another human being in the world knows about the rotting stench of this kind of pain and is not standing by accusing you of making up the whole thing. Someone else knows. Someone else believes you. And someone else understands that it did happen to you, even if the person or persons who made you their victim deny their guilt and call you a liar.

The woman who . . .

has just learned that her now twenty-five-year-old

daughter was raped as a child. The information paralyzes the mother. Not only has she learned of her daughter's rape but she discovers that her own son did the raping. "Brother raping his sister?" the mother whispers to me, her eyes wide open with revulsion and horror.

Another mother has just learned of her husband's incest many years ago with their daughter. When the mother asks the daughter, "Why didn't you tell me or anyone what was happening?" her daughter, like so many victims before her, answers, "I didn't think anyone would believe me." After all, her father is a fine upstanding Christian man. Another daughter wrote, "My parents accuse me of lying [about my father's sexual abuse] and they hold prayer meetings in their home to pray for me. They believe I'm demon-possessed." These daughters are right. No one believes them.

You may be like . . .

The woman who . . .

wrote me, reminding me of a radio interview I did on my syndicated program with Barbara Johnson. With her husband Bill, Barbara leads Spatula Ministries, which reaches out to parents of gays. The woman writing me had instantly identified with Barbara's mission in life because her son David was gay. For years now this mother has received love and nonjudgmental support from Spatula's monthly newsletters, and in writing about Barbara's loving caring spirit, the woman says:

> She [Barbara] was the only other person I knew who was going through the same thing (and then I only knew her by letter). Needless to say, there aren't support groups in churches for parents of gays or the gays themselves—even in the world—

but then, I wouldn't have gone to any type of support group at that time. So Barbara and the Lord became my lifeline.

In the last part of this woman's letter, she tells me that years ago she'd read my book on death and dying, *Mourning Song*. And then she sends this mother's heart into a tailspin of grief for her and other mothers when she tells me that, in the spring of last year, she read *Mourning Song* again. It was just after her dear son, David, died of AIDS.

I recognize the terrible price Barbara Johnson paid for Spatula Ministries, but I see Jesus in her face. And I thank God for the countless cups of cold water she's given in his name by her talks, books, letters, and phone calls. She is beautiful in her healing care of parents and families of the gay community and to many people each year who suffer and die of AIDS.

The woman who . . .

is on a first-name basis with homosexuality. She fears being terminally ill and is experiencing the raw pain of rejection because she is a lesbian. A homosexual living, working, and trying to find meaning in life in a heterosexual society. Who can she turn to? If she wants help to change her life, is she bold enough to ask a Barbara Johnson? If not, how can she deal with the ongoing struggle within her? Dare she tell anybody at her church? Probably not.

The woman who . . .

cannot conceive. She longs for a child. She dreams of it, she takes on each and every fertility plan. She seeks others' advice, medical remedies, old wives' tales, and is willing to try anything, willing to go to incredible lengths because she wants to bring a baby into the world. She would endure eight miscarriages, like one woman I know, all in the hope of "maybe next time." Or she may choose to adopt, like another woman I know very well, who adopted a little girl and found great joy in her. Yet, still, she feels like a second-class mother when she hears other mothers say or imply that since she is not a birth mother, she really doesn't come up to their "mother-of-the-year" standards.

Hear the words of this mother, a woman stricken by the infertility problem, yet gifted in putting her heart on paper, as you can tell by this prayer-poem she penned:

Oh, Father—
>   you know my usual prevailing prayer—
>   that somehow,
>   some way,
you'll surmount the obstacles of my infertility
>   and allow me to experience pregnancy and child-
birth
>   for myself.

And Lord,
>   you know I'm usually not one to bargain with you.
>   But a thought came to me today . . .
>   Maybe you're tired of my prevailing prayer—
>   (I can't say I'd blame you, if that's the case!)

>   Well,
>   then.
I'll exchange it for another—
I'll strike a deal with you, Lord,
and the stakes are high . . .

>   You see,
two of my favorite people on earth
are both stricken with the same disease.
You know them both, Father, so well—

and they know you so well.
They've both shown me real love,
your love,
in so many ways . . .
It seems odd that they've never met one another.
But what I want to say, Lord,
is that if you'll touch them both—
and take away the scourge of the crippling
disease they share—
If you'll, somehow, restore the health of their
bodies;
and let them move freely,
If you'll cause a major medical breakthrough to occur,
or simply just a major miracle—
then I'll give up on my usual prevailing prayer.
I'll close the dream-womb of my heart,
with all its persistent begging to bear a child—
If, Lord, if . . .
Then I'll shut up about my infertility—
because, Lord,
it's really more important for me to see them made
whole
than it is
to be whole myself.

Yet . . .
Out of the storm of my turbulent thoughts,
I hear a voice . . .
Telling me that God can't be bargained
with,
That we in our finiteness can't begin to change
some things
that simply just are . . .
Nor can we know each "why" behind our trials.
So,
Sometimes quiet acceptance is our only an-
swer . . .
My only answer.

And maybe that's partly why these two are so special—
>   so real—
>   so loving.

> I can learn from them . . .
>   As "prevailing prayers" give way
>   To calm acceptance.

Tracy L. Hastings

The woman who . . .

has a handicapped child. She feels great pain not because of her dear son Cory, who is brain damaged and
who acts and responds as a three year old though his
biological age is eleven, but because of others. Well-
meaning people, maybe, but people, nevertheless, who
taunt her with all kinds of suggestions from merely
thoughtless and insensitive ideas to positively stupid remarks. These words cut deep into her soul. They are not
pearls of wisdom but are downright mean—even untrue
—statements. Feel her heart pain in her letter:

> I know also, how very cruel people can be—even
> fellow Christians. I had a minister inform me that
> it was all my fault Cory was retarded. That I must
> have done something terrible in my life to have
> had a son like him.

> So I know, in a way what it feels like when ev-
> eryone you felt you could turn to 'turns on you.'
> By the way, I quit church-going after that for a
> whole year.

There are many people, well-meaning and not so well-
meaning, who have absolutely dropped me to my knees
at times with their comments.

The woman who . . .

wrote me the same day she heard me speak at a large women's conference in her state. She introduced herself like this:

> I'm the Barbara who made the bookstore find me copies of all your books even though I already had them! The Barbara whose husband just left 3 weeks ago—The Barbara who is going to lose her job because I work for a Christian organization who frowns on divorce. The Barbara who is the first person for three generations to get a divorce. The Barbara whose Christian family says the divorce is all my fault. The Barbara who feels there is literally no one in my family who still loves me. I'm **that** Barbara.

The woman who . . .

became mentally ill. Occasionally, I receive a letter from someone who can articulate her life story far better than I, even though I'm known as a professional writer. The following letter speaks eloquently. Each time I've read it, I've been moved to the depths of my soul. I've left her words unedited to give you a glimpse of mental illness from this woman's heart.

> Dear Joyce,
>
> Years ago when you were going through deep pain, I've written you to comfort you. Today I want to share with you my situation and the similar grief and pain I have gone through.
>
> Recently, one of the pastors openly admitted to me that the reason they reject me is because of my mental illness. I was so hurt that I couldn't

sleep for a night and wrote down the enclosed letter.

Dear Church Family:

It's been so long I haven't talked to you about the unusual part of my life. You see, I am a handicap, a mental handicap. It's a disease that anybody can catch at any point in their life. It's a disease that is incurable but don't forget it's not contagious. It's a disease caused by traumas in that life that not many would like to recognize, not many would care, not many. It's a disease that separates me from the outside world. It's a disease that would bring more loneliness, more isolation, more cruelty. It's a disease that no one wants to catch, and no one wants to show sympathy when someone else catches it. Everybody is afraid to be ill, and even more, mentally ill. Because once a person caught it, he has no friends, no jobs, no marriage, no money, no church, and no love.

I know you don't want to catch it, you don't even want to be around with those who do. It's just too bad that I am living among you, and I've caught it. You haven't lived with handicaps before, so it's scary. What would it take to remove that fear? Don't be around with me, don't talk to me, don't play with me, don't invite me, etc. Am I that hard on you? Do I really scare you? Do I take my clothes off to embarrass you? Do I strike you? Do I hate you? Do I mistreat you? Tell me if I do, even though I am ill, I would like to have a chance to say sorry, too.

By the way, are you a Christian? I am too. Are you perfect? No, you are not perfect, neither am I. Are you going to heaven? I will be there too. Is Jesus your friend? He's mine too. Do you read the Bible? I do too. Do you go to church? Don't blame me, I go too. We have some interests in common. We have the same friend. We have the same destiny.

Then why are you so afraid, why do you shy away from me? I am a member of Christ's body, part of your body, too. There's nothing to be afraid of. Of course, I am different from you. I am outgoing, talkative, like sports, read and write, sing and dance, cook and eat, work and rest. Isn't everybody different too? But we all drink of one Spirit, one faith, one hope, and one Lord. Don't be afraid. Okay? I love, I hug. I need friends just as much as you do. I need encouragement, protection just as much as you do.

Why do you always wait for me to come to you? If the Lord was hungry, do you feed Him? If the Lord was naked, do you clothe Him? If the Lord was sitting on a wheelchair, would you push Him? Why do you have eyes and not see? Why do you have ears and not hear?

What more can I say except that the Lord loves you and I hope you would love Him, too.

The pain of this mentally handicapped woman, the pain of all the other women I've described here, and the pain of multitudes of people whom I may never meet or hear about, all of this pain is indescribable and constantly ongoing.

Here we are, Christians, practicing our faith, loving God and trying to love our fellow mankind; yet, we watch panic-stricken as God seems to propel us from one terrifying experience to another, from one disastrous relationship to another, and from one crushing trauma to another in an endless stream of pain. How is it possible, in the face of such devastation, to move on, to get on with life (as they say) or to learn to live with it (as they say)?

I earnestly believe that here is the place where our choice of attitude is absolutely crucial to our well–being, to our ability to persevere in life, and to God's restoration of our broken souls.

I could choose to resent deeply what I perceive to be God's involvement in my life or his silence. I could choose to blame Satan for the whole problem, or I could emphatically denounce and blame other people for all the agony I'm going through. However, I believe that if I do choose one of the above, I will be giving myself a lifetime guarantee of the infectious disease of bitterness which would surround my attitude with the lingering stench of revenge. Now I have to ask myself, down the road ten or fifty years from now, is that the picture I want to see of myself? Is that what I really want to be when I grow up, a bitter old woman? Will that bitterness and anger over my hurts ever help me to accomplish my mission, the one I've been called to do, so that I can one day hear the Lord's words, "Well done thou good and faithful servant"? I think not.

I could also choose to deny that I'm hurting. I could train my mind to dwell only on the positive experiences. I could bring down a curtain around the negative things so that mentally I'd be able to ignore the storm of suffering which swirls around my soul. I could choose to brag about "never having a bad day," "never becoming angry over anything," or "never having anything happen that makes me cry or double up in pain." However, this is nothing but denial in one of its worst forms.

Whenever we push away or store our anger and our

hurts down inside us, we wear down our emotions and our energy for living. The writer, John Powell, observed that when he repressed his emotions, his stomach kept score. Funny thing—but true! So if I go the denial route, I may be mapping out a treacherous future physically, mentally, emotionally, or all three. This, too, then is an unhealthy choice.

Or I could choose the attitude for my life that my heart for months now, no, maybe for the last couple of years, has been trying to tell me. I am convinced that I must choose with no obvious or seeable evidence to believe by pure faith that I can trust God to bring me from survival to recovery. I must choose to believe the Lord can untangle the bands of steel which tightly constrict my mind and emotions because I am so wounded and broken of spirit and bring me through to wholeness and wellness.

In the early sixties, when I was about to begin my first daily fifteen-minute radio broadcast in California, my mother gave me a rather large, heavy box, which turned into a wonderful treasure trove, full of stories, poems, and newspaper articles. I've dug into her amazing collection many times over the years and have found it to hold one great illustration after another.

From that box came the teacup story. Although it's a bit of fantasy, because teacups don't really talk—not even hand-painted, English bone china cups—still, it's a charming story. It is a bit of prose which gently pushed me in the right direction, toward moving and doing something about accepting my hurts and choosing healing attitudes about the mysterious problems of suffering pain.

This is a story of an American couple who went to
England . . .
   celebrating their 25th wedding
     anniversary.
Both the man and his wife were fanciers of
   antiques . . . pottery . . . and china, so they decided to
   find something as a memento for their anniver-
sary.
When they came to Sussex . . . they passed a little
china shop.

They instantaneously stopped . . . backed up . . .
and went in.
Their eyes singled out a lovely English, hand-painted
teacup.
   "May I see that?" the man asked.
   "I've never seen a teacup like it."
   "It's beautiful!" said the woman.

Then the teacup spoke up, "Wait a minute!"
   "You don't understand . . . I haven't always been
a teacup
   and I certainly wasn't beautiful!
   "There was a time that I was red . . . and a time
when I was clay.
My master took me and rolled me . . .
and patted me over . . . and over . . . and over.
I yelled out: 'Let me alone!'
But he only smiled and said: 'Not yet.'

   "Then I was placed on a spinning wheel . . . ,"
the teacup said.
"Suddenly I was spun around . . . and around . . .
and around.
'Stop it . . . I'm getting dizzy!' I screamed.
The master only nodded and said: 'Not yet!'

   "Then he put me in an oven . . . I've never felt
such heat.
I wondered why he wanted to burn me . . . and I

yelled . . . and I knocked at the door. I could see
him through the opening . . . and I could read his
lips
as he shook his head:
'Not yet!'

"Finally the door did open . . . whew!
He put me up on the shelf . . . and I began to
cool.
'There . . . that's better,' I said.

"Then suddenly he brushed me . . . and painted
me all over.
The fumes were horrible . . . and I thought I
would gag.
'Stop it . . . stop it!' I cried.
"He only nodded: 'Not yet.'

"Then suddenly he put me back into an
oven . . .
not the first one . . . but one twice as hot.
I knew I would suffocate.
I begged . . . I pleaded . . . I screamed . . . I
cried.

"All the time I could see him through the
opening . . . nodding his head and saying:
'Not yet.'

Then I knew there was no hope . . .
and I would never make it.
I was ready to give up. But the door opened . . .
and he took me out . . .
and he placed me on a shelf.

One hour later . . . he handed me a mirror and
said:
'Look at yourself.'

"And I did . . . and I said:
'That's not me . . . it couldn't be me!
I'm not beautiful.'
'I want you to remember,' my master said,

'I know it hurt to be rolled and patted . . .
but if I had left you . . . you would have dried up.
I know it made you dizzy to spin you
around on the wheel . . .
but if I had stopped . . . you would have
crumbled.
I know it hurt . . . and it was hot and
disagreeable in the oven . . .
but if I hadn't put you there . . .
you would have cracked.
I know the fumes were bad when I brushed you . . .
and painted you all over,
But you see . . .
if I hadn't done that . . . you would never have
hardened and there would have been no color to
your life.
And if I hadn't put you back in that second
oven . . .
you would not have survived for very long . . .
and the hardness would not have held.
'Now . . . ' said the master, 'You're beautiful,
and you're what I had in mind when I first began
with you!' "

—Author Unknown

I believe that when we've been terribly hurt, we think
the wounding process has disfigured us. Certainly we do
not think of ourselves as beautiful after we have been
torn apart! Funny thing though, as this charming story
points out, the painful shaping, the rolling, patting,
painting, and firing truly make us become what God had
in mind all along—beautiful.

Of course, it is definitely natural to hurt all over when
rolled, patted, spun around, nearly burned to death in
fiery ovens, or when breathing toxic fumes. Boy, does it

hurt! No argument there from me! But though it is natural to *feel* the pain of life, it can become just as natural for us to train ourselves to see that all during our lifetime, what looks like a worst-case scenario plan of God turns out, time and time again, to produce the maximum of significant developments in our life.

These horribly painful and shattering events are the very things that add substance to our character. Even when we think we've had enough "substance," our hurts still heighten and deepen our relationships with mankind and with God. These hurts are born out of all those "awfully frightful" plans God has mapped out for us. In short, what I perceive to be God's worst for my life is often really his best. He, the master potter, designs, shapes, and brings us into being, from clay to the exquisite English teacup he saw from the beginning.

Seeing God as sovereign, as our God who has planned out our days for us, or as our master designer and loving, caring heavenly Father, doesn't come with natural ease. Our mind's computer may be programmed so that we can't admit that God is in the business of making something extraordinarily beautiful out of our lives; yet, we cling to the belief that everything that is good, lovely, or wonderful—success, good health, and the relative absence of problems—comes from God, and everything that is bad, malignant, or painful—cancer, bankruptcy, or losses of any kind—comes from Satan.

Where is this concept written? Nothing is ever *that* black or white. To praise God only for the good in our lives or to blame Satan for each evil experience is a far cry from any kind of balanced Christianity. This way of thinking can be a real stumbling block in our walk with the Lord and in our choice to accept hurts.

I believe in the God who sees the beginning from the end, who sets each of us in the center of life's milieu. This is a life where sometimes our days are peaceful, filled with brilliant sunshine, blue skies, and fleecy white clouds. However, it is a life in which, on other days we will find ourselves in the black center of a storm's darkest holocaust. Still, our God is with us. Still, our God carries out his plan for us. Still, our God leads or propels us (as my friend Clare would say) through all the twisting and turning days of our lives. He, and he alone, knows the intensity and the duration of both the joy of good times and the pain of bad times. I have no idea why God works in this way. I only know that I can trust his judgment. I can trust in those "plans" he made for me while I was being formed in my mother's womb. If indeed, as Psalm 139 assures us, God has planned out our days, it stands to reason that, besides not being surprised by the pain or the bad things that do happen to us, God does not stand idly by while Satan annihilates us.

Another earthly concept about God relative to pain disturbs me. It's probably a holdover from the 1930s sermons on hell, fire, and damnation preached by every fresh-faced Bible college or seminary graduate to the eldest of pastors. This particular God-concept conjures up a picture of the Lord sitting on his throne in heaven, rubbing his hands together, just almost itching for us to sin or to fail, or at least waiting for us to act the fool so he can take us to the proverbial woodshed and beat the living stuffings out of us. Thereby, he can teach us a lesson we won't forget.

No, no, no.

God's plan for his children as set out in the Old and the New Testaments of his word says exactly the opposite. Over and over again, when you and I are in the midst of a storm of horrible things, we need to remind ourselves that we are children of God and he is not our enemy. He is not willfully, deliberately, almost gleefully out to win the "gotcha" game. He is not plotting our demise or designing cruel and senseless events to crush and flatten us to prove he is God or to prove we can be broken. No.

God has our best, not our worst, interests in mind as he keeps us in the mainstream of life. The truth is . . . life hurts.

David wrote these words:

Though I am surrounded by troubles, you will bring me safely through them. You will clench your fist against my angry enemies! Your power will save me. The Lord will work out his plans for my life—for your lovingkindness, Lord, continues forever. Don't abandon me—for you made me.

O Lord, YOU have examined my heart and know everything about me. You know when I sit or stand. When far away you know my every thought. You chart the path ahead of me, and tell me where to stop and rest. Every moment, you know where I am. You know what I am going say before I even say it. You both precede and follow me, and place your hand of blessing on my head.

(Ps. 138:7–8; 139:1–5 LB)

Our God and David's God are one in the same. We love and serve the God who gives us his purest, his finest, twenty-four-carat best for our lives. He gave us those experiences, circumstances, and relational encounters before we were ever born. God did not plan and program our lives in order to punish or torture us. No, rather God planned to be available to us so he could lead us through those dark valleys of pain. He knows the whole of our life and he knows what he's doing . . . which is turning red clay into a work of art . . . shimmering with meaning and beauty.

I've said all that to say this. When hurts come, and they *will* come, we do have some options. We have some choices and those choices will determine not only our attitude but also the whole spectrum of our lives. Look at the wide range of attitudes.

As I've looked in wonder at the healing methods of God, I've become very aware of some logical steps which are needed if you or I are ever to accept our hurts and go on to live and tell about it, or in a word or two, survive and recover.

Here is the first step as I see it:
We must recognize that if we are ever going to live and breathe and experience some semblance of wholeness on this planet, we will have to admit to the awful reality that sometimes, more than we dreamed or would like to admit, it is downright painful to be alive.

Life hurts. It's been this way since Adam and Eve. It will be this way until we stand on the *other* side of heaven's gates. While we live here we shall suffer and bear the pain of life's wounding process.

After many years of dealing with loss and pain in her own life, my friend the author, Barbara Johnson, has told me and many other hurting people that she's recognized there is a pattern in pain, a pattern which repeats itself. She believes that when we are in severe pain, first we panic; then we suffer; and finally, we recover. Barbara's hard-won observations are so true! There is hope, but we may never get past the pain, panic, and suffering to that wonderful word *recovery* if we refuse to deal with our wounds and continue to deny their existence.

As a new knife of pain slices into my inner being, I turn back to the old prophet Habakkuk. That wonderful man took a whole chapter to write out his frustrations to God about the wounding process he saw going on all about him. He went through the patterns that Barbara talked of: He panicked; he suffered; but he ended the last chapter of his book with the first dawning light of his recovery.

> *Though the fig tree should not blossom,*
> *And there be no fruit on the vines,*
> *Though the yield of the olive should fail,*
> *And the fields produce no food,*
> *Though the flock should be cut off from the fold,*
> *And there be no cattle in the stalls,*
> *Yet I will exult in the* LORD,
> *I will rejoice in the God of my salvation.*
> *The* Lord GOD *is my strength,*
> *And He has made my feet like hinds' feet,*
> *And makes me walk on my high places.*

(Hab. 3:17–19 NAS)

It is unhealthy to deny or cover up intense pain. So when I take the first step of admitting that I am wounded, I can finally be free to scream for the help I so desperately need.

It's obvious that the second step is: Seeking help from God.

Unfortunately, there are no guided tours to lead us to

the right person, the right church, the right counselor, the right seminar, or the right therapy program to strengthen us as we deal with the long process of recovery. But I believe with all my soul that the healing of our hurts start with asking God to be the primary physician-in-charge. (We'll get second opinions from others whether we want them or not.) God can and will administer and oversee our care and he specializes in our problem area, giving the help we need the most.

The Gatlin Brothers's music album *Pure 'n Simple* has a song on it called "Healin' Stream." The bridge in the middle of that song says:

> So if your heart's been spoken to,
> And you need a new heart from above,
> Dear Friend, all I say to you is
> Just wade right out in the middle
> of the healin' stream of love.[2]

To me, wading out in the healing stream of God's love means going to him, laying the brokenness of my life before him and with faith, even the size of a mustard seed, believing that God does know what he's doing. We may not know or understand but he does.

When . . . I wade out into that healing stream . . . God puts his finger on the hemorrhaging places. . . .

I can rest in safety knowing that whatever I'm facing—the hurts of the past, its bad memories and dreadful encounters, the sins and mistakes of my life, the intense pain of the losses right now, or the fears I have concerning my future and the coming battles and wars out there—God is in charge. He is with me. He is with you. He is with us to pour out his best on us. He's here now even during a severed relationship, cancer, bankruptcy, divorce, sexual, physical or emotional abuse, or heavy grief losses. God is available. He will take care of us. Our part is to wade out into the healing stream of God's love by faith, *seeking* his help.

Not too long after I discovered and began singing Larry Gatlin's song "Healin' Stream," Francis and I were at St. Giles Presbyterian Church in Richmond, Virginia, on a Sunday morning after a weekend of speaking. During the song service, we sang the old hymn, "Jesus Keep Me Near the Cross." When we got to the chorus, Francis looked at me and without words we both knew that the next time I sang "Healin' Stream," I'd add these great lines from the old hymn:

> "Jesus, keep me near the cross,
> There a precious fountain
> *Free to all—a healing stream,*
> Flows from Calv'ry's mountain."

When I take the initiative, when I make the choice to accept my hurts—risky as that may seem—and I wade out into that healing stream . . . God puts his finger on the hemorrhaging places of pain in me and stops the bleeding, bringing a measure of healing. Or I find that when I bring a burning issue to God, a fire which has been raging within me, he douses me with an outpouring of his love from his healing stream and the hot embers within me begin to die out. Or God eases my emotional strain and stress, and even sometimes erases it, to replace it with his peace. Almost mysteriously, God begins a healing. God works it out, and rarely do I understand his timing or just how he has done it.

These journeys with God's healing love give me courage to believe that whatever we're going through, whatever is strangling us this very moment, he will surround us with the evidence of his care, his grace, and his healing stream of love.

I remember being in love with a picture in my childhood. It was a painting of a mother bird on her nest with her babies peeking out here and there from underneath her. But the tree branches which held her nest hung over a raging torrent of a flood-swollen river. All around the mother and her babies was the evidence of a devastating wind storm; yet, calmly she remained on her nest.

The picture was titled *Peace*. It enthralled my spirit and imagination many times. But now that I'm older, as I think of it, I believe I would have given it a different title. It was a picture of peace amidst the storm, but because of what I know of my own mind-set and of God's healing ways, I'd call the picture *Trusting*. The mother bird, amidst the impending destruction and doom, was trusting, trusting that in spite of everything, all *would be well*.

God really has planned out our days and years

too. He wants us to live the abundant life as he promised in John 1:10. If he does this for me, just one of his children, he will do it for you, another one of his children.

Again, an old hymn creeps into the hurting places of my mind and soul. Do you remember these oft-sung lyrics?

> Be not dismayed whate'er betide,
> God will take care of you;
> Beneath His wings of love abide,
> God will take care of you.

Those truthful and beautiful words bring me to the third step:

Watch for the people God works through to help us survive and move on to recovery. After we have admitted that we are wounded and hurting, and after we seek help from our caring heavenly Father, we need constantly to train ourselves to be watchful and alert for the people, the ways, the means, and the opportunities God brings to us which surprise us with healing for our brokenness.

The shepherd in the Psalms said of God, "He restores my soul." It's been my experience that sometimes when God restores my soul, he does it directly by speaking to my heart. His gentle spirit will whisper a passage of scripture during a sleepless night in the dark just before the dawn and in my mind I hear,

> *Be at rest once more, O my soul,*
> *for the* Lord *has been good to you.*

(Ps. 116:7 NIV)

Or I hear,

> *"[F]or I am with you to save you*
> *And deliver you," says the* LORD.

(Jer. 15:20 RSV)

Or,

> *Praise be to the* LORD,
> for he showed his wonderful love to me
> when I was in a besieged city.
> In my alarm I said,
> "I am cut off from your sight!"
> Yet you heard my cry for mercy
> when I called to you for help."

(Ps. 31:21–22 NIV)

But many more times than I can remember or recall, God has helped me to accept my hurts, to heal, to move to recovery, and to carry out the passion and mission of my life by working through other people. Over and over again, God works through my brothers and sisters in Christ. They write a letter, they call, or they give a hug that helps me to hold together when I am unraveling and am beside myself with anxiety, pain, or just old-fashioned loneliness.

As I related in *Unworld People,* when I was in the holocaust of pain after my divorce, a few people like the Wigginses family, Charles Rice, a pastor in the United Methodist Church, began reaching out to me. My friend Clare Bauer pushed past my dazed state of shock and phoned me every Monday morning from her home in California. I was so numb that sometimes I couldn't talk. Other times, I couldn't hear. Still other times, nothing she said made sense to me; yet, she kept up her phone calls.

My children took their precious vacation weeks to travel to Texas to spend time with me. One or two Texas friends came out to my cabin by the lake. I remember little of what was said, but I do know they came and they held my broken heart in their hands.

Then, from all over the country, people somehow found my address and wrote to me. Amazingly, hundreds of letters came from people I'd never met. During that time, their letters ministered to me. It was a dramatic revelation to me of how God works through others to heal brokenness. My debt of gratitude to God and to all those loving souls is enormous. My word to you is for you to watch for his mysterious ways of bringing restoration by working through some of his children.

God shone through others like this woman. Just recently, she wrote to me, recalling the time right after I'd moved to Texas from California. Her letter is pure "balcony person," and in one part she wrote:

> I want you to know that even though you don't know me, that you have touched my life in so many special ways. When you were living at Lake Mexia, you came into the church office to talk with Pastor Charles Rice. At the time, I had no idea that you were going through such terrible battles in your life. But when you entered my office, your pain entered also. When I looked into your eyes . . . though they were smiling and gentle on the outside . . . I felt as though I looked into your soul and saw the pain. You never knew it, but while you were counseling with (Pastor) Charles, I prayed in the outer office that God would enfold you in his loving arms and still the

pain. It wasn't until weeks later, when you spoke at our ladies circle at our brunch, that you shared some of the pain with our small group. And my heart broke for you again. I have thought about you so very many times since then and you have been in my prayers more often than I could understand why.

During my early days in Texas, even though I was out of the long stretches of massive headaches due to a TMJ dysfunction, my occlusion and joint damage was in need of serious repair. I remembered back in 1981, when a wonderful Catholic priest prayed with me. He asked God to let me find the "root causes" of my TMJ, and in due course, that prayer was answered. God then worked through a dentist, Dr. Stephen Cutbirth. And despite the fact that I'd had around eighteen dentists, this caring and gifted young man correctly diagnosed my problem, accessed the damage, and adroitly reconstructed my occlusion so that, though I'll probably always be a TMJ patient, I am no longer in that unbearable and constant pain. In fact, I'm about ninety-eight percent pain free. God works through his children.

A number of months after Francis and I were married, we moved from the lovely seclusion of the cabin at Lake Mexia and the warmth of people like the Wigginses and Pastor Rice to a larger city. There, I began to experience rejection as I'd never dreamed possible. I could feel myself coming closer to the dark edge of madness and wondering just how long it would be before I lost what little I felt was left of my mind.

God, my husband, Francis, my children, and a few select friends were the only ones who really knew and understood just how deep the anguishing pain and growing depression of my soul was becoming. So it is no wonder that it was Francis, who was closest to me, who found and arranged for me to see a psychologist.

From the first five minutes of Dr. Will Pannabecker's initial visit, God began a new healing process. For eight months this skilled and godly Christian doctor came to our home each week. And because of the intensive-care therapy he provided for both of us, we survived. I survived. It was as if God provided the right person for us at the most precarious and fragile time of our lives and snatched us back in time.

I suspect that God arranged for that great doctor to be in our town just for us because at the end of those eight months, Dr. Pannabecker accepted the directorship of a hospital and he and his wife moved to the Northeast. We have never been the same since, and we know Dr. Pannabecker was a vital part in saving our sanity and our lives.

I feel certain God will provide the ''people-help'' you need just as he did for us. He is a God who does supply our deepest needs. Again, I repeat, watch for the ''balcony people'' because God will work through them for your wholeness and restoration. These people, friends, counselors, pastors, or a particular member of your family become wonderful agents of healing and reconciliation in our lives. I do think that God stands back a bit, smiling in great approving love, as the hurting and the healers he has chosen to use come together as he planned.

Perhaps while I'm talking about healing from the emotional pain of our lives, I should explain one facet of my own struggle with pain because I am unwilling (in the case of my divorce) and unable (in the case of Christian leadership's response to it) to fully describe the levels of pain as I could if I were writing about the physical pain of TMJ. I'm certain that many of you may think that I'm overreacting or at least overstating the skinning process which produced an intensity of pain like I never dreamed. But if you have experienced the unbelievable, the thing that could "never happen to me," or the unrelenting, ongoing wounding process in its full measure, then you know I'm not exaggerating. It is to you to whom I write of watching for the beautiful people God will choose to work through for our hope and our wholeness.

Occasionally God works through a person we may only see once in our lifetime. One such woman comes to mind. She touched my life once, briefly, for a few minutes. Her words were not only an answer to my anguished prayer but directly responsible for pulling me across the line of choosing the acceptance route in regard to my hurts.

For the year Francis and I lived in this particular town, the woman jogged past our home each day. I had no idea that God had a lovely plan involving her in my life or the enormous contribution she would make to us.

The rejection that year from many Christians was virtually impossible to ignore or to work around. That same year my father died and though God had restored our relationship (which I wrote about in *Irregular People and Unworld People*), it was a long and hideous year. The pressure and the stress levels of living in that town kept escalating. Francis and I finally decided that it was time to sell our home and move. It must have been God's time too; for though the real estate market was duck-down soft, our house sold within four days of our putting it on the market to the first people who walked through it.

One morning, while our home was still in escrow, and just after our realtor tacked the SOLD card up to our front yard sign, I received a most devastating phone call. I was told about a woman in our town who was saying some pretty vicious things about me to a number of people both in this town and to people in other cities across the country.

I'll never forget that morning—for despite the friends, the family, the wonderful letters from balcony people, the dentistry of Dr. Cutbirth, and the therapy of Dr. Pannabecker, the information I'd been given made me feel like all the life support systems I once had to keep me alive had just been unplugged.

I stumbled into our breakfast room, collapsed into my rocking chair, and cried out my newest agony to God. First, I begged him to take me home to be with him. Then, I asked why . . . why . . . why . . . ?

Later, I just sat there, crying and sobbing out my anger and frustration. When I was still feeling stunned but a bit more rational, I said aloud, "Lord, isn't there one Christian in this whole town who will show us your love? Isn't there one Christian woman who will be kind to me?" (I'd have settled for just civil, much less kind.) "Or," I went on, "am I just requesting an impossible dream? Is there anybody here who will admit their slightly judgmental and unchristian behavior toward us?"

Of course, I knew there were a dozen or so people who lived in that town who had not been judgmental or critical and who, to this day, are dear and precious friends. But sitting there in my rocking chair that awful morning, I felt like my life was in the middle of an exploding war zone and that there was not one single human being in the whole world who cared.

Blindly, I went back to asking God, "Is there one Christian who just might say, 'I'm sorry, Joyce, for the pain we've added to your life.'" More specifically, I begged, "Isn't there one brother or sister in the family of God who will reach out to us right now, today?" I wept, prayed and wept some more.

I sat in that rocker for hours. My emotions careened from seething anger at the woman who was bad-mouthing me, and then at anyone who would listen, to fearing I'd lose my mind instead of dying. I felt paralyzed by the present circumstances and almost paranoid of the unknown. If I lived through this and remained somewhat sane, where would we go? How would we live? Would this kind of rejection never end? These and other questions jabbed and taunted my soul.

But God. Oh yes, God. He had a unique, once-in-a-lifetime surprise in store for me that afternoon, though I had no way of knowing it then. I wasn't at all sure he was listening to the outpouring of my heart. I should have known better. But often, when you're standing in the fiery furnace, it's hard to see the Lord standing right next to you in the flames.

Since I couldn't seem to stop the continuous flow of tears, I finally left the rocking chair and just roamed around our home in a numb trance. Much later that afternoon I found myself in the living room, absentmindedly playing the piano. In my life music has often bridged the gap between raw pain and partial healing. Slowly, I became aware that I had repeated two or three times a tune that had sung itself in my head.

I pulled myself together as best I could and composed a few lyrics to the melody. Then, in a dull state of apathy, I began to sing the song. Just as I was about to jot it down on paper, I glanced up and out of our living room window. I could see a woman dressed in a jogging outfit, standing out front of our house studying the real estate sign.

I thought she was going to resume her run. Instead, she turned with slow, determined steps, and stunned me by walking up our curved driveway toward our front door. During the year we had lived there, only our kids and one or two local people ever visited us. I was glued to the piano bench, unable to comprehend the fact that this woman was actually coming to my house.

I'd seen her many times before as she jogged on the road in front of our house, but she'd never slowed, much less stopped or even returned the traditional Texas "howdy" I waved at her. Certainly, she had never come up our driveway.

Now, she rang our doorbell!

Opening the door, I offered, "Ah, hello?"

The two of us stood there for a second or two. Then, without any preamble, introduction, or hello, she looked at me and uttered the most amazing speech. Words came out of her that just that morning I had prayed and wished for but never fully believed I would hear.

Abruptly, she came to the point. "I come to you in the name of Jesus Christ. I beg your forgiveness. I've jogged past your house for over a year now, knowing you lived here." She took a deep breath.

"The first time I went by your house the Lord told me to come to your door. I was to tell you that he loves you and that I love you. But I refused. I said, 'No, I'm not going to stop my run. She's divorced and remarried, and I'm not going to have anything to do with her.' "

The woman looked up at our home and glanced around at the magnificent hundred-year-old oak trees, which spread their branches over our yard. Then, looking back at me, she continued, "All this year, each time I jogged past your house the Lord has asked me to give you this message. But I've always said, 'No.'

"A few months ago, I told the group of women in my Bible study class at church that you lived on my road. I also told them what God kept repeatedly asking me to tell you. I asked them what they thought. Should I stop and tell Joyce Landorf Heatherley about God's love and mine?

"Absolutely not, they agreed. I shouldn't bother with you because of your 'circumstances.' So until today I've never stopped or given you this message."

I was still trying to get my lungs back to normal breathing patterns again and frantically trying to assimilate at least a part of this astonishing confrontation. But all I could think of as I studied her face was that I thought she was the most beautiful woman in all of Texas. I managed to tell her so, but she brushed aside my remark with a shake of her head.

Looking at me with tears in her eyes and genuine remorse in her voice, she said, "When I saw the SOLD sign just now, I finally realized what we have done. We've run you out of this town haven't we?"

I nodded, but before I could speak she said, "Can you ever forgive us?"

That precious woman may never know (unless she reads it here) just how unique God's healing ways are toward his children, how special she was to me, or how deeply she touched my heart and spirit during our brief encounter at my front door.

I felt quite incapable of saying anything at all. But I did understand that because of this beautiful woman, it would be right and incredibly appropriate for me to forgive not only her but the whole town. Vigorously, I nodded my head. Then, remembering my manners, I asked her to come inside—begged her to please come inside.

She shook her head no and left me speechless again by explaining, "I can't come in. . . . I don't deserve to set foot inside your home. I've done a terrible thing to you. I was wrong in refusing to speak to you. Just please forgive me and the people of this town."

I felt as if I had just been notified that I'd won a million dollars on one of those impossible-to-win publishers sweepstakes deals. That very morning, I'd felt like I was dying. That afternoon, while most of my bones were still broken, at least I was up and on my feet again. The woman's words and spirit were impossible to ignore or to explain away.

As I stood there looking at this precious Christian woman who did what our heavenly Father wanted her to do (who cares if she was a little late?), I was overwhelmed with the comfort, the hope, and the joy of our conversation. To think that the God I serve and love had, for one of the worst years of my life, asked one of his children, my sister in the body of Christ, to give me the message of his love and hers was indescribable! To see this woman, to hear her message and her request was a most humbling moment for me.

She had become that one Christian person I'd so desperately prayed for just hours before. She was that one human being, that one "balcony person" in the whole town, who had reached out to me and become the spokesperson for all the other Christians. Today, she had been wonderfully obedient to the still, small voice of the Holy Spirit when she stopped her run. She had spoken the only words I so desperately wanted and dearly needed to hear. That woman picked me up, as it were, from where I was lying face down in the dirt, dusted me off with her kind touching message, and lifted me to my feet. It was she who helped me to take my first halting steps in resuming the race I knew I must run.

I know this woman at my front door was used of God to pull me across the starting line of accepting my hurts and watching for the people God uses in our recovery. Yet, I never saw her again.

Dear, broken and hurting child of God, watch for God's intervention. Remember too, God may ask one of his children to comfort you, to care for you, or to minister to you in some way, and for reasons only they may know, the child of God says no. But watch for those rare and exceedingly beautiful people who God urges to walk up your driveway to knock on your door . . . even if it's later than you thought it should be. Watch. Watch for that one Christian human being who comes to you in the nick of time like a well-trained paramedic. The one who brings life-saving equipment. The one who gives you emotional oxygen so you can breathe again. The one who takes your vital signs. The one who administers healing medication as needed. The one who, by his or her loving, encouraging words, rushes you into the intensive care unit, where God can continue the healing and recovery process in your life and where, as the Psalmist promised, God can restore your soul, saving and delivering you from the hideousness of life's most brutal wounds.

Some of you may be shaking your head. I can hear your protest. And I can hear the weariness of your heart when you say, "But Joyce, of the two people who have hurt me the most in my lifetime—one is gone and the other is dead. How can I choose to accept the damage they did and have a healthy attitude . . . or even begin to watch for how God will work through others for my wholeness?"

Your voice touches down deeply in my own heart. Many times I have asked myself and my heavenly Father, "What about hurts inflicted by people who are no longer with me? Can they reach out across a continent or up from their grave and continue their harmful battering of my soul and spirit?"

Just this past weekend, after I'd spoken to a small group of pastors' wives, one of the women told me about a lady in her prayer and Bible study group. She described the woman as being a very nice lady but one whose attitudes were negative and often critical.

It seemed that the woman constantly blamed everything on her parents' failure to meet her needs when she was a child. The woman, now in her forties, with both parents dead, was still analyzing and rehashing the agonizing hurts of her childhood.

"How can I help her to get beyond the devastation she suffered with her parents?" the pastor's wife asked.

How indeed? Can people reach across time and space inflicting pain on us even after they're gone? I know it feels like they can, but from my own counseling sessions and extensive reading, I do not believe we are dealing with the facts here. We are dealing with our feelings, valid feelings. But the truth is those people and the terrible relationships we had with them really can't hurt us anymore. So what do we do when we are controlled by our past? What do we do with our feelings and our emotional pain?

When one human being has hurt another human being and the relationship is over—either because of death, divorce, or distance—we will never be able to accept our hurts and watch for the ways people and God work through them for our healing as long as we hang on to the people and circumstances of those particular hurts.

This is nothing new. Years ago, as I sat in my mother's kitchen, she prayed for me, asking God for a healing of my memories. After that, it was up to me to let go of those painful memories, to close the door on those memories and say good-bye without looking back.

Today, I firmly believe my mother held a "releasing ceremony" for me right there in her kitchen. The idea for a "releasing ceremony" was not original with my mother or with me. I came upon it in a paper by Robert E. Elliott, "A Theology of Divorce" (written for Perkins School of Theology). His concept and mine are not precisely the same, but in reading his paper, the need for a "releasing ceremony" became very clear to me.

Hearing about the woman who seemed in desperate need of some kind of release from the tenacious grip of her parents and her past, I suggested to the pastor's wife and to several other women who were standing around us, a "releasing ceremony." They all nodded their heads; and even though I'd not talked of this concept publicly before, I could tell by their affirming looks and my pounding heart that we just might be on the right track.

Such a ceremony would probably be best done with a loving, praying friend or with a mother like mine. But if you are alone, as I am right now, or if you have no loved one close by in your life right now, then here is how I see the ceremony taking place. In fact, because of some newly opened scars within me, this is exactly what I've done here, as I sit at my dining room table writing this. Within the privacy of your mind . . .

1. Take yourself to a comforting place. A place you love. A place where you feel unthreatened and very safe.

2. Visualize not only the people who have hurt you, but also the Lord. Look at the people before you and know they cannot touch or reach for you, for you are shielded by God from anymore harm. The Lord stands between you and them.

3. Begin by genuinely thanking the people for anything positive you can remember about them: a few good times, some special or fun occasion, beloved children, other relatives or friends this relationship gave to you. But find *something* to thank them for so you can give them at least an ounce of grace or a moment of saving face.

4. Without elaborating, state that you are sorry for harm you have caused them. I started to write, "State that you are sorry for any harm you *may* have caused them," but as I thought it over, whether it's directly, indirectly, or inadvertently, we have all caused some harm to happen in this relationship.

5. Look at the person or the persons in the eye and, as kindly as you can, tell them that you are releasing them from this relationship. Tell them that you both are

free to leave now. Then, as gently as possible, tell them "good–bye." Release them. Let them go.

6. Finally, walk away from the ceremony. You can leave without guilt or shame. You leave knowing you have done the responsible thing and that, in doing it, you have brought closure to the past hurts of this relationship. You leave with God's blessing.

7. Don't look back. Look ahead. Expect God to go before you. Watch for the healing of your emotions.

If you do choose to have a ceremony such as I have just described, I wish I could be with you. But I can't. No one can. Neither can I begin to predict how or when God will work in your behalf for your particular hurts. But by sharing the way he has worked in my life and in other's lives, I can confidently assure you that our heavenly Father sees even the smallest painful need in the lives of all his children. And I wonder, even if you *are* alone, if it's possible right now, as you're reading these pages, that our great and loving God is about to do an extraordinary work toward restoring your broken spirit? He sees your heart and mine when we reach out for his help, and in his time, he lovingly comes to our aid. There is a verse in the third chapter of Ecclesiastes which reassures us of this: "He has made everything beautiful in its time" (Ecc. 3:11 RSV). In his time, God can make even ugly relationships, past or present, beautiful.

Let's say we have just gone through the releasing ceremony. We are now experiencing the first breath of freedom that can come from closure. We are feeling the release from the pressure of the previous burden of pain, and we can rest knowing that for our part, we have entrusted it into God's hands.

But may I take this one step further? We know that

there are some things in life which are never explained to us, some relationships which are never fully resolved, and some questions which are never dealt with, much less answered. I can accept the releasing ceremony as one of the ways God enables me as I live on this earth to help myself to move further along toward healing and wholeness. But what about when we get to heaven? What about the people of those shattered relationships, especially the Christians?

Even after we have *mentally* mended things, I have to ask, what will it be like to be in heaven with them? Will they greet me on one of those golden streets as one former publisher of mine did in a department store? He acted as if he had never written me a hateful letter, as if he'd had lunch with Francis and me last Tuesday, and as if every bad experience with us had completely vanished from his mind, or perhaps not even happened in the first place. These good Christian men and women are still part of my pain. What happens in heaven?

I can just see myself in heaven, coming out on my front porch on my first day there only to discover that my neighbors on both sides of me are the "used-to-be close" friends who rejected, hurt or refused to speak to me while I lived on this earth.

What are they going to do? Shrug their shoulders and say, "There goes the neighborhood." And how will they respond when I wave at them and say, "Hi. Betcha never thought you'd see me up here. Fooled ya, didn't I?"

Up until last year, I treated this casually, with humor, but now I can't limit my response to that. It's too large a question in my mind and in the minds of others for me to lightly toss it off. Revelation 21:4 tells us that in heaven "the former things are passed away." But how? Won't it still hurt to see them there?

During a two-hour layover at an airport terminal, a good friend was telling me about her mother's illness. She believed both of her parents' deaths were imminent.

Her parents loved the Lord, and her father had been a minister most of his life. I was pretty confident that they would be in heaven, but I also knew something else. My friend's father had sexually molested her and her sisters, and though her mother had known about it, she had made no apparent effort to stop it or even to acknowledge it had ever happened. The father denied everything and accused his daughters of lying. My friend and her father had been estranged for many years.

"How will you feel or act when you see your parents, especially your dad, in heaven?" I asked. What I was really wondering was how will any of us feel, react, or respond when we see someone on the other shore who has given us or others great pain with no resolution in this life. I asked, "What do you think it will be like to see him walking around heaven?" It sounded pretty unjust and unfair, somehow, for my friend's father (or anyone else) to deny the guilt of his actions while on earth and then walk around heaven smiling and chatting with the very people he hurt as if nothing ever happened.

"It's going to be all right," my friend said quietly and gently. I was stunned and wondered how? An insightful and sensitive woman, she then told me this story.

She had had a dream or a vision; she couldn't say which it was. She didn't even know if it was from God or a product of her own creative imagination. But recently as she had been contemplating her parents' age and their physical condition, she found herself wondering what it would be like to be in heaven with her father after so many years of not seeing or talking with him here on earth. She described the scene which had unfolded before her eyes.

In her mind's eye, her father had just died, and she saw him as he left the earth, went up into the sky, and walked through heaven's gates. However, just as he crossed heaven's threshold, an angel stepped out in front of him, took his arm, and said, "Come over here and sit down. I have some things I must tell you."

She watched her father being seated by the angel and then listened in astonishment as the angel began listing, in chronological order, all the things her father had done. It was a detailed report on each harmful act her father had ever committed in his life, including the incest he had committed with his daughters. The angel never missed a thing. My friend said what was amazing was that her father sat there listening intently. He never interrupted. He never objected. He never tried to explain or excuse his actions. He never defended himself, and never once did he try to deny the awful truth. He just sat there listening to the angel, nodding his head, his face wet from weeping. Just as it looked as if he couldn't stand any more charges, the angel finished.

My friend watched as the angel reached over, patted the man's shoulder, and uttered these incredibly astounding words, "But everything is all right now. It's all taken care of . . . it's all right now."

"Immediately," she said, "my father got up and walked over by the gates. He just stood there as if he was waiting for someone before he ventured any farther into heaven. And I knew instantly who he was waiting for. It was me.''

Then her dream changed and she said, "Suddenly I saw myself dying and moving toward heaven. When I reached the gate, my father was still right there, his arms outstretched toward me, and he was calling me by my name. I ran to him and he took me in his arms and hugged me. He told me of his love for me. He welcomed me as his daughter, and I had no need to hear an apology from him because somehow God and the angel had made it all right!''

I've no idea if this is actually going to be the method or the way God will reconcile us to each other in heaven. But it sounds just like God.

Jesus introduced most of his parables by saying, "The kingdom of God is like . . ." Perhaps my friend's dream or vision was really a present-day parable to let us understand a little better how "the former things will all be passed away" and how the kingdom of God really will be. It's just like our heavenly Father who understands our need for full-circle restoration to commission an angel to set the record straight! This also gives new meaning to a verse in the Psalms which says, "For the Angel of the Lord guards and rescues all who reverence him" (Ps 34:7 LB). It's just like God to have his angels deliver us from our most dreaded fears and our worst hurts.

Many times since my friend related this intriguing scenario to me, I have walked myself through it, putting in my own list of characters. Who knows? Just perhaps, when I die and go to heaven and before I get very far past those pearly gates, an angel will step out, take my arm, sit me down, and say, "Joyce-Honey, I have some things I must tell you."

Until a better explanation comes along, I'm choosing this one as my first choice for those people and those painful relationships that are not able to be reconciled while we are here on this earth. But it doesn't matter exactly how God accomplishes this. The scriptures tell us that he will wipe away our tears in heaven and there will be no pain or suffering or even night there. So I'm confident that he must have a wonderful plan. I'm confident that our hurts which have been so grievous and the people who gave them to us so hateful, plus all the hurts we have inflicted on others, God will, in his way and time, make beautiful!

Charles Reynolds Brown wrote almost a hundred years ago:

> God is a God who knows that we have need of all things that are demanded for joyous and useful experience; a Friend who does not suffer even a sparrow to fall to the ground without His notice; a Father who is more ready to hear and answer the prayerful appeals of His people than earthly fathers are to give bread to their children; an All-embracing Providence whose affectionate interest in our well-being counts the very hairs on our heads![3]

Knowing that God can be trusted, let's not allow anything to hinder us from choosing to have a great and healthy attitude about our hurts.

Someone once said that, "Happiness is not the absence of conflict, but the ability to deal with it." I believe this begins at the level of our will and power to choose our attitude. David knew the exacting truth of this all through his life. When David was weary of his enemies' constant attacks, he decided to take action in regard to his attitude about those wounds. Time and again he stated the words, "I will." And he knew who to trust. "When I am afraid, I will trust in you" (Ps. 56:3 NIV).

God will take our hurts, as incredibly painful and deep as they are, and guide us across the chasm of pain to recovery. Remember, trusting God can mean watching for the people and for the variety of ways he works through others for our wholeness. He does it by methods which never dawn on us until it's over and we find ourselves wide-eyed with wonder. Breathlessly, we repeat Amy Carmichael's lines:

> Thou hast called me . . . I cannot tell why.
> Thou wilt justify me . . . I cannot tell how.
> Thou wilt glorify me . . . I cannot tell when.[4]

And in great joy we can shout with the Psalmist to others around us and to our own needy souls, "Come, see the glorious things God has done. What marvelous miracles happen to his people!" (Ps. 66:5 LB).

FOUR

I CHOOSE TO PUT AWAY MY BLUE BLANKET . . .

The supermarket was about five blocks away from my home. There was nothing particularly religious or educating about the large building or its busy parking lot, the even busier management people, checkers, or the box boys (except for one box boy, a teenager, my wonderful son Rick). But that particular grocery store served me well for a number of years, not only with nourishment and all those nonfood products I always bought but as a resource of a number of very special lessons. As I recall, some of my very best material was acted out right in front of me and my unyielding grocery cart, like some rare new art form of a dramatic play. More often than I can remember, as I observed those one-, two-, or three-

115

act performances unfolding, I was enlightened or encouraged or given some unexpected tutelage on the intricate and fascinating ways of people and their relationships.

This incident at that store, as you may recall from reading *The Richest Lady in Town* (Austin, TX: Balcony, 1991), happened late one Saturday afternoon. Naturally, I had put off the job of grocery shopping for as long as I could. We all know about the time it takes, the expense involved, and the horrible fact that when we get our grocery bags home, our work has only just begun. It never stops.

We still face the long routine of carrying it all in, washing the produce and putting everything away. Then we have to take it all out of the fridge or the cupboards again, prepare and cook it, do something with the leftovers, clean up the kitchen, take out the trash, and then —then, we get to start the whole process all over again. AUUUGH! But back to that Saturday.

There couldn't have been a worse time to shop. Furthermore, I hadn't been able to con anyone into coming with me to push the basket or at least to give me moral support as I spent all that time and money. So there I was, impatiently alone and trying to push my cart through the streaming throng of shoppers.

It was the only cart that was left. One wheel went south and the other due east, and everyone before me had abandoned it. I decided to pull myself together and try to keep in mind that the main priority here was to get the shopping done in the shortest amount of time possible.

I was concentrating so hard, going down each aisle, writing out menus in my head, and trying to race the clock that I almost failed to notice I was making absolutely no headway.

The roadblock was just ahead of me. She was a young woman and I couldn't get around her no matter how hard I tried to outmaneuver her cart. She had her two darling sons with her. One must have been four or five and the other probably not quite two. It required no course in Psychology 101 to ascertain that from the top of her supersized pink rollers in her hair, down to her sandals, this near hysterical mother was just quite possibly going to go "crackers," as the British say.

I imagined her story like this.

All week she'd tried to find time to shampoo her hair and do her nails (preferably alone, without one of the little people asking, "What are you doing?") but as all mothers of young children understand, she'd run out of time. So, earlier today, I was guessing, she decided that she'd clean up the house, and after the kids were in bed tonight, she'd give herself some TLC with bath and shampoo time. Tomorrow, she'd do her grocery shopping.

However, I fantasized, just a few moments ago, her husband phoned and said, "Honey, I know this is short notice but it's important. I've invited the boss and his wife over for dinner tonight."

I could imagine her standing there, staring first at the phone in her hand and then at one of her boys who was gleefully pouring a white trail of milk on the floor for the dog who was joyously lapping it up, and I could hear her mumble, "Are you serious? Tonight?"

At least, that's how I called it because she was about as calm and collected as a volcano getting ready to erupt.

Her boys, on the other hand, were having the most delightful time of their lives! You could just tell they had been cooped up all week and this coming to the grocery store with both of them riding in the front seat of the cart was a Big Deal, almost as good as a new ride at Disneyland.

They were tickled pink to be there, thrilled to "help" their mother. They handed her a can here and a box of cookies there. I could tell she was trying not to scream as she put each item back on the first available shelf space she found. (I could see my son Rick stocking shelves later and the puzzled look on his face, wondering how that sack of sugar made it across two aisles and ended up beside the dill pickles.)

The boys climbed in and out of their seat in the cart and once the littlest one started to get into my basket. I handed him back to his mother and said, "I believe this belongs to you?" Nary a word passed her lips as she took him back and rolled her eyes toward the ceiling in the traditional mother's gesture of helplessness.

Both of us had worked our way down several aisles and were almost halfway through the store. By now, I was in more of a hurry than ever, but no matter how hard or how persistent I was in trying to get past her, I just couldn't do it.

As we headed for the wide meat aisle, hope soared within me. "Aha!" I thought. "I'll cut her off at the pass!" So I maneuvered, raced, picked up less meat than I had planned, grabbed a few pieces of fruit in the produce department and sprinted through shoppers in my cross-store marathon, with my head lowered for action and my cart sailing along. (Well, actually with those wheels, the cart didn't *sail* along; it just felt that way.)

Into the final lap, I dashed, right up to the front of the store and made it to the checkout! Instantly, other customers formed a line behind me. The store was jammed with rush-hour shoppers.

I hardly had time to congratulate myself on having made it to the finish line when I looked up, and lo and behold, there in line, right in front of me, was the young mother and her two boys. So much for my great maneuvering!

I figured I shouldn't fight it, so I practiced a few deep-breathing relaxation techniques and resigned myself to waiting my turn. However, someone invisible tapped me on the shoulder, and I heard in my head, "Pay attention." I wasn't too sure if that was a "God-suggestion" or a "Joyce-suggestion," but I paid attention, just in case.

About then, it happened. The youngest boy in the cart ahead of me had apparently run out of inspiring things to do because he was playing a new game. He was tugging on the tall wire rack beside him, which was loaded with candy, gum, and tons of other goodies. I'm not sure what tantalizing thoughts raced through his little mind, but he looked as if he'd decided he needed a little more action in his life. With all his little might, he gave the rack a very healthy yank and pulled the whole thing over, showering him and his brother with a fantastic rainfull of candy.

It was every kid's dream come true. Both boys were delighted!

As the rack began its fall, it hooked itself onto another one filled with a jillion candy bars. The two racks meshed and toppled down together, doubling the treasure and spraying gum, Lifesavers™, cough drops, Rolaids™, and giant Peter Paul Almond Joy™ bars over the area around the cash register. One-sixteenth of a second later, the volcano I mentioned earlier did indeed erupt into a hot molten mass of hysterical screaming. All of which, need I tell you, was directed at the petrified boys.

We were all knee-deep in candy bars, and it caused pandemonium all over the store. The mother went noticeably berserk. She was wild-eyed, crying and frantically yelling, "What am I going to do? How could this happen to me? I can't believe this whole mess. Do I have to pay for it?"

A deep male voice came over the intercom speakers. "Code four . . . code four . . . code four." Personnel came running from every direction. The manager, meat packers, their assistants, produce people, clerks and box boys all flew toward the front of the store, geared for action. They seemed to know this was no drill! At this same moment (we all know that word of mouth is the best advertisement), kids were telling other kids about this wonderful natural disaster. Soon, gangs of kids were running into the store, stuffing candy in their pockets and racing for the outer doors. Customers were rolling around in Rolaids™ and crushing candy bars to death and my feet were hidden in a sea of Lifesavers™ and Dentyne™ gum.

By now, the volcano was pouring a hot torrid stream of big words, hissing words, bad words, and small threatening words into the four little ears still sitting in the cart below her. Apparently, even after she called them by their first, middle, and last names, she still didn't think she was getting through. So she thundered down at them, grabbing one boy by his sweater collar and the other by one shoulder, and tried to swoop them up to eye level, an arm's length away from her face, where she could verbally let them have it.

I say "tried to lift them up." Have you ever tried to pull a kid out of a grocery cart? Yes? Then, you know that if they think they're "gonna git it," they lock their legs around the basket seat so when you try to bring them out, you lift up the cart with them. Imagine trying to get two legs untangled, much less four! For a second there, I thought she was going to have to break bones, but she finally freed them both and shook those terrified boys until I was sure blood would come spurting out of any convenient opening. After a final violent shake for emphasis, the volcano slammed them down on the floor yelling, "Now, shut up and don't you move!"

They stood frozen, like two little soldiers in ramrod positions, no color in their faces, their eyes peeled open in astonished horror.

Bedlam still reigned in the store. But, I'll give her credit, the mother turned from the boys, and even though she was still hysterical and crying uncontrollably, she pulled herself together and started helping the clean-up crew.

Slowly, I came out of shock and was about to move to help also when, out of the corner of my eye (I couldn't believe it), I saw the littlest boy *move. Oh darling child*, I thought, *don't do that or your mother is going to snap you in two like a fresh green bean.* We are talking total destruction.

Never taking his eyes off his mother's face, the boy began inching backward, and with one hand, he searched the air behind him until he found what he wanted—her large open straw handbag. Warily eyeing his mother, he pulled out a small, faded blue blanket. As he moved back to his mark on the floor, he tucked the tattered remnants of that blanket firmly under his chin, and almost instantly, his tense shoulders relaxed and lowered. He breathed a loud sigh and color returned to his face. Tranquility spread over him, erasing the fear from his eyes, and he began to sway from side to side ever so gently, humming a little tune.

I was enchanted by this peaceful little boy and the way his blanket had brought such pleasure and serenity to his face. I felt as if the Lord whispered down some corridor of my mind, "Did you see that?" When the child's whole world crashed down around him, when everything went wrong, when his very life was in jeopardy, he did not reach for his mother but for the only thing that would make everything all right: his faded blue blanket. He was gentled by its presence.

I thought that Saturday afternoon, and have thought many times since then, that his faded blue blanket had probably never given him a moment of pain, never a teeth-rattling, head-shaking, brain-jarring lecture. In fact, that blue blanket had probably never given him anything but joy and comfort, except perhaps when he lost it to the washing machine and didn't find it until his mother took it out of the dryer.

There in the grocery store, he sought, found, and hugged his blanket, and the broken pieces of his world clicked silently back into place.

Over the years of observing my children and grand-children and many other children, as well, with their "blue blankets," I've noticed that blue blankets are not necessarily brand new or without holes and tears. Usu-ally, they are neither very clean nor one whit loved be-cause of their beauty or their gorgeous condition. No siree! Mostly, blue blankets are like the bedraggled skin horse of *The Velveteen Rabbit,* whose hide and skin had been dearly loved and hugged off of him. And when blue blankets come up missing, there is great gnashing of teeth and heartrending tears until the prized blanket is found.

Most of us parents fondly and knowingly smile when we remember the noteworthy episodes we have had with our children's blue blankets. And any child who has ever dragged one around á la Linus in the *Peanuts* cartoon— whether it was a blanket, a stuffed teddy bear, a soft toy— knows exactly how valuable this blanket is to his or her own peace of mind and overall security.

When my now very grown-up fourteen-year-old grand-daughter, April Joy, was a mere eighteen months old, she, like most children, gave her blanket a name, Dee-Dee. April's mother, Teresa, an extraordinary English teacher, taught her many other words at the time, in-cluding the important word *potty.* But our whole family noticed that whenever April Joy was scared, fearful, or felt in any way threatened, she'd put her entire vocabu-lary into play. I can still hear her in the car one day when we swerved and narrowly avoided a head-on collision. She was in the back seat, and in her sweet but frightened-to-death little voice, she cried, "Mommie, Dee Dee, potty . . . Mommie, Dee Dee, potty . . ."

Sometimes we adults believe we have lost all our need for a blue blanket now that we are grown-ups. We reason that, for crying out loud, we'd look fairly stupid grabbing for and carrying our tattered blue blanket around the house, to our job, to church, or to our kids' soccer games. After all, we're not two years old anymore.

But is it all that cut and dried?

When we become adults, do we lose this basic need for

comfort and security? I doubt it. But we feel as if we're now supposed to have grown out of that stage and the older we get, the less we are supposed to act like a child.

Francis and I were disappointedly sitting out a two-hour delay in Atlanta's mega airport. Our connecting flight to Austin, Texas, had been canceled. We were both dead tired. We'd been on the road several days on a speaking tour, and we just wanted to get home. I could feel my tiredness trying to get together with the nausea I'd been feeling for several hours. If that had transpired, I would have thrown up all over everybody and gone on a crying jag that probably still wouldn't be over.

As we sat waiting, a man walked slowly by us dragging his obviously very tired son behind him. The four or five year old was sobbing his heart out and pleading his case with his father.

"Daddy . . . I'm tired. . . . I wanna go home. . . . Let's go back. Why can't we get on the airplane? Daaaaadddy . . . ?"

Perhaps the father had explained (more than ten times) why they had to wait, but by now the man was in no mood to go over that again. So he just held his son's hand and pulled the reluctant child down the concourse. The father broke his own boredom by reading the ads on the wall displays and, other than holding the boy's hand, seemed fairly oblivious to the boy's presence or pleading. I was feeling very connected to the child because I identified with his desire to go home.

Suddenly, the five year old raised his voice and plaintively squalled out, "I'm tired! I'm not going anywhere!" With that proclamation, he pulled his hand free of his dad's and just fell, tummy down on the floor.

In a heartbeat, I knew how he felt. He'd had it. He

didn't care what his dad or the other people around thought of him. He didn't care that passengers in the corridor were stepping over his lifeless form and rushing on to catch their flights. The boy made it perfectly clear. Nothing was going to make him get up and take one more step.

The very preoccupied dad now noticed his son, but of course, he had no other choice. He tried to scoop his son off the carpet, but the boy played limp wet noodle. Those of us watching the father's efforts found it an amusing spectacle, though I doubt the father found anything faintly funny about the situation.

As I absorbed the whole scene before me, I found myself wishing I was five years old. Wishing I could refuse to go on. Wishing I could lie down beside that kid and wail out my tired frustrations about traveling. I wished I could use his method of protest and put an end to this very unsatisfactory afternoon by throwing myself down on the floor. But the awful truth is I'm not that little boy. I'm not five years old or younger. I've grown up (supposedly), and because I'm an adult, I'm not free to act or behave like a child. I tried to ignore St. Paul's words when they abruptly popped up in my mind, but I couldn't:

> It's like this: when I was a child I spoke and thought and reasoned as a child does. But when I became a man my thoughts grew far beyond those of my childhood, and now I have put away the childish things (1 Cor. 13:11 LB).

Ironically, when it feels like the painful realities of life are coming at me head-on like a freight train and my little light is about to be snuffed out, I revert ever so quickly to my childhood. Believe me, I sincerely long for the soft, safe, comforting folds of my blue blanket. Oh yes, I know we grown-ups are not *supposed* to want our blankets, but the truth is, I do. I suspect you do too.

> *I know we grown-ups are not* supposed *to want our blankets, but . . . I do.*

We can all feel for children who are distressed and wanting their blue blankets. I can still feel the little boy's relief in the grocery store amidst all the ruckus he'd caused as he reached for and found his blue blanket.

I can feel April's fear and vulnerability as she verbally reached out from the back seat of the car for her blue blanket.

I can feel the five year old's defeat and frustration in the airport as he flopped to the floor, making it his temporary blue blanket.

And as I see myself in these children, I realize that we do not outgrow our need for security, our need for comfort, our need for gentling, our need for someone to please just understand, our need for healing and wholeness. We just trade in our child's small faded blue blanket for a larger adult's blue blanket.

Here are some times I think we grown-ups reach for our blue blankets of comfort.

When we fear what is happening right now.

When we sense we've lost all control in our life because of death, divorce or forced separation from loved ones.

When we suffer major pain, physically or emotionally.

When we lose our job, face bankruptcy or watch finances disappear.

When we are threatened by transition and change which seems to be happening in every single arena of our lives.

When we feel absolutely no emotional support from the loved one closest to us.

When we see that we are all alone, ignored or abandoned by our friends.

When we can't stand *anymore* pain.

When we are convinced that no one on God's green earth understands that pain, or even cares.

When there's no easing or tapering off of our loneliness.

When we feel trapped and can see no hope of things ever changing.

Believe me, any or all of the above combined can send us by the most direct route to our very own blue blanket whether we are two or ninety-two years old.

You could probably write your own list of anxieties which have sent you scurrying to grab your blue blanket, or as Dr. Pannabecker called mine, your "escape hatch."

I can readily see the truth in this catchy little saying (one of hundreds Barb Johnson has sent me over the years), for it spells out our need to have an adult blue blanket:

Sometimes, just when things look the bleakest,
You have to look life squarely in the eye and say,

"Go ahead, life . . . take your best shot . . .
I can take whatever you dish out."
Other times, it's best to just go to bed
With a really good book, a big plate of fudge
And a box full of donuts!

I think there are very few people living under, or in the midst of, today's stress and pressure who don't have a blue blanket or two. Some may deny it or refuse to admit it, but I suspect most of us, when frightened or hurting, run pell–mell for that particular escape hatch of ours and desperately clutch our favorite blue blanket to our hearts.

Perhaps you are pulling away from these printed words because you think and feel that surely anyone who is a real child of God would never (or rarely) have any need for a blue blanket. Best you think again.

Even King David had a blue blanket. Running all through the Psalms one can see David's oft-repeated request and need for his own blue blanket. He longed to find and hold this blanket. He called it "wings of a dove." Hear the terror of David's thoughts in Psalm 55, when he was faced with another onslaught of devastation, when the pain of his life was once more intolerable.

LISTEN TO MY prayer, O God; don't hide yourself when I cry to you. Hear me, Lord! Listen to me! For I groan and weep beneath my burden of woe. My enemies shout against me and threaten me with death. They surround me with terror and plot to kill me. Their fury and hatred rise to engulf me. My heart is in anguish within me. Stark fear overpowers me. Trembling and horror overwhelm me. Oh, for wings like a dove, to fly away and rest! I would fly to the far off deserts and stay there. I would flee to some refuge from all this storm (Ps. 55:1–8 LB).

Beloved David, we do hear your anguished plea for the wings of a dove. We identify with your longing to flee and your frantic desire to find some safe refuge from the storms that were battering your life. We know. We know.

Through his pain and his desire to fly away and hide, David was learning some very disquieting things about being a king, about being in leadership, about having relationships with God and mankind and about the high cost of being obedient and growing. I'm sure David found it excruciatingly lonely at the top. Read Psalm 88 and see David's preoccupation with his battle with loneliness. He would naturally reach for the warmth and comfort of his blue blanket, believing that if he could just "fly away," he'd leave loneliness behind.

I'm sure, too, that David realized the hard way, by tough experiences, that he who takes a public position becomes a highly visible target, an easy mark. His enemies, perhaps like yours and mine, were always just one heartbeat behind him. His soul and even his bones, like ours, must have been incredibly weary. No wonder David, wonderfully human like us, longed to escape somewhere until the storm passed. He yearned like those of us in leadership positions to find some distant desert where, in total privacy, he could repair and recover without the prying eyes of others.

Again and again, David desperately pleads with God to give him his blue blanket, his escape hatch, and that place where he can get away from the glaring intensity of people, enemies, and pain. I'm sure of this because of the many passages of scripture where David begs the

Lord to ''rescue'' him. Psalm 69 is filled with this cry of his, and the cry echoes over and over again because David, all grown up, the king of all the Israelites, *needed* his blue blanket. He often expressed his desperate desire to fly away, to disappear, and his clear desire to find some solace and comfort away from the source of his pain.

There's little, if any, difference between our need for a blue blanket and David's. Now, our blue blankets may not share exact descriptions, so let me list some of the blue blankets I've heard about, including the name of my own. These are true-to-life blue blankets, common escape hatches. They are what we long to have, tucked under our chin, when the pain of what is happening right now is very scary or growing by the nanoseconds, downright unbearable.

Sometimes a blue blanket is simple to identify and is relatively harmless to you or someone else. Other blue blankets are very dangerous. They are hidden escapes and agendas. They are well-kept secrets of ours, not easily detected by others. These menacing blue blankets can become entrenched in our daily lives until they encroach disastrously on our lives and consume us or others. It is paramount to lay aside these perilous blue blankets. I give you this list so that we can examine and learn not only about our own blue blanket but about the blue blankets of others.

THE BLUE BLANKET OF SLEEP

The young newly divorced single mother unveiled her secret blue blanket to me in a word: *sleeping*.

Quietly, she confessed that she went to bed whenever

she needed to escape the overwhelming pain of the responsibility of financially supporting herself and her children. To escape, she would go to bed. Often for hours at
a time, she slept, leaving her two preschool children in
front of a TV with a VCR movie running.

She wasn't reaching for her blue blanket out of anger
toward her former husband, or society in general, nor
was she trying to act in a potentially dangerous or fool-
hardy way. She was in pure despair. Sleeping was her
escape route.

We talked of some of the alternatives and choices
open to her. Primarily, in our brief time together, we
spoke of ways she could begin to lay aside her potentially
harmful blue blanket. One option was that when she felt
the financial pressure building and the panic attack closing in, she would choose to sleep only when her little
ones were napping. I reminded her that all mothers with
little ones were perpetually tired and very much in need
of naps themselves.

The mother of Charles and John Wesley had twenty-
one children. Each day she reserved one hour alone for
prayer, instructing that no one was allowed to disturb
her. I have a sneaking suspicion that in between praying
for her children, she managed an occasional nap. (At
least, with twenty-one children that's how I would have
done it.)

Another option the young mother and I talked about
was that she try reducing the amount of time she slept a
little each day.

I'm not a professional psychologist and my instant
sidewalk counseling is certainly not long–term therapy,
but I believe we must lay aside our blue blankets that

could be destructive to others, even when we ourselves can barely stand the pain.

When the young mother and I parted, I felt she had made up her mind to make good choices and to take her first, shaky and tentative steps toward laying aside her blue blanket of sleeping. She'd begun to realize that she had choices, and her face reflected that her inner attitudes had gone from panicked depression to a small measure of hopefulness.

THE BLUE BLANKET OF READING OR WATCHING TV

I have to admit that I am a passionate and zealous reader. My unquenchable love of books, part of the inheritance my mother gave me, runs deep and fervidly within me. Reading could be my blue blanket, because if I was ever in the enviable position of having nothing to do (not likely in my lifetime on this planet), I'd lie on a beach and read, read, read.

I am not only a reader but a writer as well, and I'm heavily into stories which deal with the truth concerning the vast subject of life and relationships. I'm also into stories wherever I can find them. Books, theatrical plays, operas, sermons, interviews, and (despite my upbringing which forbade me to go to the show) movies, which brings me to another love of mine: television. Television, since its emergence into our homes in the late forties, has continually received bad press from the pulpits of our land (much like radio did in its early days). But the beauty and the pleasure of watching TV lies in the hand holding the remote control unit. So for me, movies and television could also be blue blankets. That these aren't

problems to me is no credit to my intelligence or spiritu-
ality. Rather, I feel guilty if I read books when I have a
deadline and am supposed to be writing books instead of
reading them. And I have found with TV that there's
only a little time at night to watch, and Francis and I are
practically gifted with a remote control unit.

But I can easily understand how both of these activities
could control my life if I used them as blue blankets for
my escape from reality. I've talked with many of you who
see this blue blanket as a monopolizing time stealer and
a potentially difficult habit to break, even after the pain
has abated and a blue blanket is not as urgently needed.

Again, what I suggest here is laying aside this or any
other blue blanket, which is destructive to our souls or a
dictator of our life's priorities.

THE BLUE BLANKET OF EATING OR NOT EATING

Often when I talk privately with a person about her
blue blanket, she almost immediately blurts out the
name of what she eats or how she starves herself when
she feels stress closing in on her or when chronic pain or
depression knocks the hope out of her and brings her to
her knees.

"Chocolates!" from a twenty-seven-year-old high
school teacher.

"Junk food, all kinds!" from a business associate.

"Food in general!" from a movie star.

"Donuts," from me.

My mother, brother, and sister all knew that in times
of crisis, my dad would head for the refrigerator. But
even without a crisis, I noticed that Dad always timed his
visits to me during the lunch or dinner hour, and in his

later years as he'd walk into my house, his first question after the briefest of hellos was, "Got any cold juice?" Eventually, if I knew he was coming, I'd have cold juice ready and waiting. But we all just accepted that in stressful or nonstressful situations, Dad ate.

Whenever my mother or I was hospitalized, we'd look at each other and ask, "Where's dad?" We'd smile, and then say together, "In the cafeteria." Naturally.

If we don't abuse this blue blanket, it can serve us well. We are all comforted and sustained by food or by eating together with someone we love. The ancient ceremony of breaking bread is still necessary and wonderful.

My memory is rich with times when I was in kindergarten in Battle Creek, Michigan. My mother and I stayed with Grandma Miller, my father's Irish mother, while he was away in evangelistic meetings with the evangelist C. M. Ward. My grandma firmly believed that 90 percent of the world's ills could be cured by sitting down (me on her lap) and sharing a cup of hot tea laced with milk and sugar.

During another year of my dad's traveling, my mother and I lived in Highland Park, Michigan, with my Hungarian Grandma Uzon. Now she believed that 90 percent of the world's ills could be cured by eating. Period. But what I loved the most was that she'd sit down (me on her lap) and share her cups of coffee, gloriously delicious with cream or canned condensed milk and four teaspoons, at least, of sugar. It was a great and lovely blue blanket.

Lovely that is, unless it were to become a compulsive way of life.

When our weight balloons, our cholesterol rockets skyward, our hearts are endangered by fat and our self-esteem disappears, food becomes a life-threatening blue blanket. And for our health's sake, we must deal with it and choose to lay it aside.

When we eat or when we don't eat (as with a compulsive eater versus an anorexic or bulimic patient), we are physically and mentally in denial about the pain and truth of our lives. This blue blanket helps us to walk away from conflicts or confrontations. It becomes our refusal to see our life as it really is. It could become a life-threatening problem.

I'm not professionally adroit enough to diagnose the seriousness of the problems of over- or undereating, and I can't begin to lay out the steps to help you choose to put down your blue blanket. But others can. And if your blue blanket, no matter how secret or how innocent it looks, is controlling your life, you need help. Go for it. Go to a qualified counselor or to a program, but go. Go to someone you can trust.

THE BLUE BLANKET OF TELEPHONING

I never knew her last name nor did I ever meet her in person, but in the early 1970s a woman called me long distance from a pay phone in a suburb of Los Angeles, California. She called to talk with me every day and eventually several times a day for a solid six months.

Our conversations always ran the same. She told me how bad Christians had treated her. She was unable to hear my remarks so she just repeated her statement about Christians and how they had let her down.

In those daily phone calls, filled with street and traffic

noise and sometimes the sound of wind or rainfall, I was never able to get her to tell me anything about herself or her life's circumstances. Even my attempts to set up correspondence with her so I could write to her or send her books failed as she would never give me her address. But I kept answering my phone because I felt I should answer and respond to her calls. She had value as a human being. She was another child of God, and I could almost hear the bleak, cold sound of her loneliness pouring through the phone lines. It was easy to sense that emotionally she was very fragile.

After six months of phoning me, she stepped up the number of calls a day until I became emotionally fragile. My efforts to get her to seek help repeatedly failed and my family life suffered. So I finally made the difficult decision to obtain an unlisted number.

I have always wished it could have been different. She was such a tormented woman, tragically addicted to that blue blanket of phoning me or someone. Why she was the way she was, how she got that way, or what drove her to that particular blue blanket, I'll probably never know. But I do understand that the people who escape their hurts by obsessive phoning are troubled and lonely souls. And sadly, they drive friends and family away precisely when they need all the friends and family they can get.

Since my first encounter with that woman, I have dealt with five or six other people who have repeatedly called me, sometimes at great expense. One woman, who eventually went for counseling about this blue blanket, told me years later: "Joyce, you must have hated to hear the phone ring during my marathon phoning days!" Then

she added, "And I hated to pay the five- and six-hun-
dred-dollar-a-month phone bills. But when I was depressed about my divorce and when I felt the world closing in, I'd call you and some other friends. I didn't even
know it was an addiction, I just ran for the phone every
time I felt overwhelmed by my crisis."

Women at my speaking engagements have often told
me of a person in their family, church, or neighborhood
who plagues them morning, noon, or night with long
involved (and tragic) phone calls. Callers who are on the
phone to you daily over long periods of time need professional help, and often, wellness and recovery happens
only after long-term therapy.

Phoning is a convenient, larger-than-life blanket for a
growing number of people who are hugless and who
struggle emotionally in our touchless society. A phone
call may very well be the only way a person reaches out or
feels any connection with others.

THE BLUE BLANKET OF BUSY-NESS

"My husband is a workaholic but even when he's
home, all he does is watch sports on TV."

"My wife is married to her job."

"My wife is never home, and when she is, she's too
busy or too tired."

"My husband never talks to me."

"My wife bores me to death with small talk."

"All my husband ever says about his day is 'fine.' "

"All my wife really loves is shopping."

"Our family never eats any meals together."

"My dad is an absentee father."

"Mom never has time to listen to us kids."

"My son or daughter never calls or visit me."

I hear these complaints frequently from everyone—kids, teenagers, young adults, and senior citizens—about their daily lives. Frankly, they are giving us some tough messages to swallow about the roots of isolation and estrangement within many of yesterday's, today's, and tomorrow's families.

. . . there are no easy and quick answers . . . no "they just ride-off-into-the-sunset-and-live-happily-ever-after" endings.

It is not my intention here to use these quotes (or some of the others I routinely hear) as if they represent the only problems in the home, nor do I mean ever to imply that this whole matter of family living is just the typical, simplistic, and trivial struggle everyone goes through . . . that it's no big deal or just a matter of adjusting, pacing oneself, or merely thinking great positive thoughts . . . no, not at all!

You'd have to be seriously dead to be unaware of the intricate complexities in today's family relationships. And I know for an absolute fact that there are no easy and quick answers . . . no instant solutions and no "they just ride-off-into-the-sunset-and-live-happily-ever-after" endings.

But perhaps it would help us all to see our relationships and family struggles by some different lights. Small lights, yes, but lights nevertheless.

Intertwined with the need to put food on the table, to provide a roof over the family's head and to produce an emotional safe harbor for our loved ones is the noisy, false countertheme of our problem with busy-ness. I see two kinds of busy-ness.

Most all of us are caught up in a normal busy-ness as it relates to our personal finances and family support systems . . . and rightly so. But if getting or making money becomes our god, "the love of money is the root of all evil" becomes far more than a biblical truism.

When we give this first kind of busy-ness a higher priority than most anything else in our family, our relationships are thwarted and never have the chance to be all God designed them to be. We may live together, but we become as ships passing in the night, vaguely aware of each other's presence but never close enough to talk or communicate. Obviously, this creates and promotes profound neglect in relationships between husbands and wives and between parents and children. Our struggles, questions and differences are left hanging, unresolved or abandoned altogether, and we sum up our family ties with a shrug of the shoulder and with the guilt of the unfinished business. Sometimes as we look back over the years, we realize we've missed the point of family life: to know, love and esteem each other's presence.

Then, in order to compensate for what we know or perceive is a dysfunctional family lifestyle, we begin the search for a blue blanket to soften the onslaught of past memories and present pain. And, guess what? Very often the blue blanket we run to find is more busy-ness to escape the ill effects of the first kind of busy-ness. It is a second kind of busy-ness designed to help us get even busier so we can escape the ill effects of busy-ness in the first place.

Plunging headlong into the blue blanket of busy-ness happens when we see clearly that we have bad relationships at home. We may have serious marital problems, conflicts with our kids or some heavy abuses from our past, but one thing we know for sure is that we can't and won't break up the home. So in an all-out effort to keep the stress levels down and the family together and survive with our sanity intact, we create our own escape route called keep busy at all costs.

Being busy eats up our waking hours, and there's no time left to deal with the real problems at hand. Sadly, this blue blanket may anesthetize our souls to the hurt that's happening in our own families. It's even possible that we've had this lifestyle for so long that we perceive it as harmless, or maybe it's so much a part of us that we don't see it at all.

Busy-ness complicates our lives because:

1. It prevents us from seeking solutions to the problem.

2. It broadens the distance and builds barriers (not bridges) between us and the members of our family.

3. But saddest of all, it gradually takes control of us and the blue blanket of busy-ness becomes our way of life, even our lifestyle.

The things we do to create busy-ness are quite harmless within themselves, but they are lethal to our relationships when they become our blue blanket. The energy we could use to deal with turbulent relationships is spent at the office or on the job after hours. We have no energy left when it comes time to go home. Or we create busy-ness by doing so many things at church or for a club or for good causes that there's no time for really hearing or seeing the needs in our own home with our spouse or our kids. Or maybe we have a hobby, like sewing or making craft items, that does not leave any time for family excursions or fun times together. Perhaps our busy-ness is a recreational activity like golf or aerobics that goes beyond fulfilling the need for exercise and relaxation and becomes a medium for "staying away" from someone or some conflict.

"But," I can hear some of you protesting, "isn't busy-ness sometimes a very logical and practical blue blanket?" We think it is logical in that it helps us stay in our homes with our families, preserving the look of wholeness, and practical because it removes us from dealing with problem relationships. But the result of this kind of busy-ness is pure destruction. It covers our emotions and removes us from the constant friction we feel from rubbing against the grain of the varied personalities of our family members. It also covers and hides some family "truths" too hideous to fathom.

When life at home does not play out "Walton" style where the family is united and everybody just loves everyone else, even to the point of not going to sleep until each member tells the other "good-night" . . . when life at home is perpetually dismal with little or no emotional warmth or stability, perhaps even–dangerously abusive . . . our busy-ness becomes our ever–present thought which is shaped in our minds by one word: *escape.*

One wonders, when life at home means relationships are, or certainly appear to be, mentally or emotionally dead, how can we continue to stay? When the arguments and stress that always accompany them drain all our energy and leave our souls exhausted, what is there to do? When we lose our ability to communicate with some of our closest kin, when relationships crack and lose their vitality or are endlessly boring or when the nest, once full, is now empty, how can we bear the loneliness which closes in over our hearts and minds like a large dark shroud? Or when life at home, or our past memories of it, are filled with hideous images because of sexual, physical, or emotional abuse, again, what can we do? Where can we run? Who can we turn to?

Can't you hear in your heart of hearts David's cry, "Oh, for wings like a dove." But alas, for most of us, especially as Christians, leaving our home, "flying away," putting distance between ourselves and volatile relationships is just not possible; it's unthinkable.

Sometimes, even when we are courageous enough to seek and find personal, family, or marital counseling, or we choose to use intervention procedures with a loved one, we shut down, overcome by the momentous threat to our own security. Often one abused sibling will not risk coming forward to collaborate with another member of the family. So rather than make waves or risk being vulnerable ourselves or make anyone in the family feel "uncomfortable," we devise and grab our own escape plan. It's a blueprint designed to guide us into busy-ness. Big time.

Busy-ness is a very effective blue blanket and can be a well-entrenched, even respectable way of life. In fact, it's so effective that we rarely have time to think in depth about what we are doing or to come to terms concerning our struggles. But I believe the most damaging thing busy-ness does to our souls is that it depletes the strength we need that's required to make decisions or to deal with the highly volatile relational conflicts at hand.

We can become workaholics, in or out of the home. Some may even applaud our efforts and point with pride to our accomplishments, labeling us "success oriented" or "self-made millionaires." But the cost of this blue blanket in terms of damage to husband, wife, kids, and other extended family members is exorbitant.

This blue blanket of busy-ness also does something subtle but nonetheless real, for it lets us stay within the framework of our home life. It allows us to keep up our respectable appearances at home, job, and church. Many times busy-ness makes it look as if our vows to protect and cherish our loved ones are all intact, even when they are unraveling. Busy-ness turns the light on above the doorway marked Exit, and whenever we escape beneath the blanket of busy-ness, we are usually walking away . . . not toward our loved ones.

The final tab is usually a dysfunctional family to one degree or another. Husband/wife, mother/father, brother/sister, grandparents end up distanced from one another, feeling unwanted, isolated, abandoned and deeply troubled. They are puzzled by their own feelings of anxiety and some suffer from self-imposed guilt.

It occurs to me that some of you may hold dear this blue blanket of busy-ness not because you don't want to deal with family conflicts but because the dysfunctions of your home were, from the beginning, products of a profoundly basic personality disorder. I know some of you who could not live without this blue blanket because those deep-seated wars of someone's life drove you away from, not toward, home.

I say this as kindly as I can: Busy-ness is never going to

be a permanent solution. If you are depending on it to get you through life, it may do that. But you will be accepting a sentence to living death.

Should your busy-ness keep you away from solvable family conflicts, I would urge you to reexamine your priorities and lifestyles. Don't wait for a life-threatening event or accident to jolt your reality awareness. Often I have read or heard of someone who is either in the final stages of cancer or who has walked away from a major airline crash or auto accident. These people make virtually the same comment: "Every day I have now is a gift. This (illness or death or accident) has changed my life. Now I see new beauty in a sunrise and I feel new joy when I kiss my baby's face. Life is precious to me now and I thank God for each new day to live as his child." Their newfound knowledge forever changes their thoughts and attitudes and, thereby, their way of living. If they had the blue blanket of busy-ness *before* their experience, they would choose to do everything they could *afterward* to lay it aside, perhaps in record time.

If we are to have a family or a home at all, some changes in attitudes and behavior patterns have to happen. We have to deliberately decide to lay aside our blue blankets of busy-ness and thoughtfully choose to see each new day as a gift and each relationship at home as very, very precious.

THE BLUE BLANKETS OF ALCOHOL, DRUGS, AND PRESCRIPTION PILLS

I haven't listed the various types of blue blankets in any specific order nor have I attempted to lay a guilt trip on any person for *having* a blue blanket. We all have one sort or another, and I'm well aware that blue blankets are our own built-in system for coping with the pain of our wounds.

But perhaps of the most destructive blue blankets around in our society today, this blue blanket could be placed at the top of the list. Addiction to alcohol, drugs, and prescription pills produces an almost certain death warrant.

Although this is not my particular blue blanket, I've talked with hundreds of people who deal or cope with addiction, either in their own lives or in the lives of loved ones. And these conversations have only underscored the need for me to understand the addict and for the desperate need of getting help to that person so he can lay aside this lethal blue blanket.

If we do not care about the addicted simply because it's not "my problem" or it's not "touching my family," we fail one of the basic tenets of Jesus' teaching—that of loving one another. Left alone to run its course, this blue blanket will continue to wipe out loved ones and families at an increasing rate each year.

Volumes have been and are being written about these venomous blue blankets. Scores of big-screen movies and television shows explore the hazards, the havoc, and the lethal toxicity of these escape routes. I believe these blue blankets are a present-day symptom of what Henri Nouwen calls our feelings of "disconnectedness" and our attempt to escape the pain of "boredom, resentment and depression."

Alcohol and substance abuse have been around a long time. We barely get into the ninth chapter of Genesis before we read, "Noah was the first tiller of the soil. He

planted a vineyard; and he drank of the wine, and became drunk" (Gen. 9:20 RSV). Although Noah may not
have been able to understand or describe in present
terms the psychological struggles within him or his emotional feeling of "disconnectedness," we do know that
his blue blanket of alcohol is as ancient and timeworn as
the Noachian flood itself.

Drugs, like opium and its derivative, heroin, are a little
newer on the historic scene than Noah, but not by much.
Dioscorides in the first century A.D. described opium very
much as we know it today, and opium poppies were well
known to the ancient Greeks, including Homer who
wrote in the *Odyssey* about the use of a drug (opium) as a
"beverage of hospitality."

The value of alcohol, drugs or prescription pills in the
medical and scientific fields is undisputed. One has only
to watch a loved one writhing in excruciating pain for a
short time to be grateful when relief finally comes by the
dripping of morphine (a chief derivative of opium)
through an intravenous tube. No one in his right mind is
against this usage.

When we stand by the bedside, we marvel at the intricate work of God. Who but God would have allowed the
red and white opium poppies to be a part of our world's
creation in the first place? He, our caring heavenly Father, made us in his image. We are his children, and as
the apostle Paul wrote, God makes *all things work together
for our good.* Even these substances? Yes. Even alcohol?
Yes.

The ancient vineyards of Noah were no accidental ex-
periment on the part of our first recorded farmer. His
planting, harvesting, and turning the grapes into wine
was not a sin. And drinking his own brew was not a sin

either, nor did it cause God to turn away from him or excise him out of the pages of the scriptures. Biblically, it is clear that ingesting alcohol was not wrong, nor did it make the drinker a bad person. Paul makes a point of telling the new Christians at Ephesus not to be drunk with wine (Eph. 5:18). Paul outlined the behavior for the deacons of the early church to Timothy. We read, "Deacons likewise must be serious, not double–tongued, not addicted to much wine" (1 Tim. 3:8 RSV). But later in the fifth chapter Paul admonishes, "No longer drink only water, but use a little wine for the sake of your stomach and your frequent ailments" (1 Tim. 5:23 RSV). The early Christians were neither to use Paul's words as a command never to drink wine or as an excuse for drinking themselves into a stupor. Being drunk and out of control and allowing a substance to play havoc with our thoughts, actions, and responses was the issue then and is the issue now.

Addiction is the name of the real killer.

This blue blanket can start innocently enough, with small increments of single or combined substances which may provide a few precious moments of relief or give us highs from the tension and stress of the hour. But it also has the unbelievable potential of being lethal to ourselves and stabbing to death the loving vitality out of our most precious relationships with others. It rapes, plunders, and violates the very core of our personhood, ultimately enslaving us and addicting us to an almost unbreakable lifestyle that can only deteriorate down a dark street whose grim sign reads Dead End.

Also, it is truly scary that we never know for sure, or at least right up front, whether we are in that "one out of twelve" (or whatever percentage it is today) who can become addicted. And what's more frightening is that unless the addict recognizes his problem and seeks help, or loved ones choose to use the intervention process, there is little chance or hope of ever being clean and free from the addiction. Sadly, the addiction not only endangers the addict's life and family relationships but the lives of future generations.

Rescuers from God come into our lives in the most dire of times.

By now, I can tell you are sick of all this bad news and are ready for the good news. Naturally, there is good news because God always has his own plans for our safety from our self-destructive blue blankets.

It should come as no surprise that when God designed "rescue and recovery operations," he would also train and provide the rescuers. He can rescue those of his children who hold tightly to this particular blue blanket. And he chooses to work through his people as he has throughout the ages.

Rescuers from God come into our lives in the most dire of times. They come in different genders and with different mission statements. But make no mistake about it, God sends them. They are missionaries such as the great Hudson Taylor, who opened up inland China to the gospel, or Florence Nightingale, who set new standards of nursing and rescued thousands of the sick and the dying.

There was Dr. Sam Shoemaker, the spiritual pioneer and seed-founder of Alcoholics Anonymous, who was one of God's great rescuers for this blue blanket. This man conceived the idea of support groups years before the idea became popular in the 1960s and 1970s. As Bruce Larson noted in the introduction of *Extraordinary Living for Ordinary Men,* "He (Sam Shoemaker) believed that two drunks who found sobriety through the power of surrender to a living Christ could start a fellowship (support group) that could help other drunks."[1] Out of that concept the "Twelve-Step" program blossomed and is still branching out, vibrantly growing, rescuing, saving, and giving people new lives and new purposes.

God commissions his children to the rescue. He works through us to save, to liberate, and to snatch the afflicted away from death's bony hand.

If our blue blanket is alcohol, drugs, or prescription pills, then I believe our first move toward wholeness is, as the greeting goes at A.A.: "Hi, my name is (fill in the blank). I am a (fill in the addiction)."

Then, listen for God's welcoming "Hi" back to us through his children. This is unconditional love in action. The tip-off that it's God who is working through his children comes from the noticeable absence of human judgment, rejection, or criticism. When love like this is practiced, blue blankets can be folded up and put away.

THE BLUE BLANKET OF ANALYZING AND AGONIZING OVER OUR PAST

Even though it was years ago, I remember the look in the woman's eyes who stood before me after one of my meetings. She had poured out a litany of grievous events

from a thirty-year span. It was full of sorrow and heartache. Her mother died when she was eleven; her college
scholarship fell through ending her dream of teaching;
her first marriage produced two children but ended in
divorce; her second marriage left her a widow; she spent
years seeking help from one counselor after another; her
teenaged son committed suicide. I wept with her and felt
helplessly inadequate to offer solutions for such overwhelming pain. The woman had suffered more than an
ordinary or normal share of tragedies. Then, suddenly, I
was aware that she was looking into my face and asking,
"Tell me what to do. Give me something to help me."

Thousands of times I've stood on this scary spot, looking into the tear-stained face of a woman, wondering
what possible help or hope I could give. But then just as
many times before—I know of no other way to explain it
—I recognized the familiar inner quickening of the Holy
Spirit in my soul, and I risked saying what I believed
needed to be said.

Sensing strongly that the woman had carried and
clutched the weighty past for so long, she was drained of
all spiritual, physical, and emotional energy and guessing
that she was emotionally fragile, I began by simply listening to her. When it was my turn, I talked with her about
some basic things I felt might comfort her and give her
some hope for recovery. In my three-point list, I gave her
(1) several suggestions, (2) a minimal maintenance plan
for her sanity, and (3) a long–term option for her future
hurts.

Perhaps I was overconfident in my counsel, or maybe I
was suffering from a touch of pride. I remember, however, being struck by the woman's response. She listened,

or at least I thought she did, and then she said, "But I wish you'd tell me one, two, three, what to do."

"But I did," I replied.

"No," she said, "I want to hear step one, step two, and step three."

"I did. I gave you one, two, three," I said again and then repeated the points.

"No, no. I want one, two, and three." And with that she walked away from me shaking her head and saying, "I wish someone would just tell me what to do."

Certainly my three-point plan or my lack of professional counseling skills may have terminated our conversation. Or maybe she was more seriously ill than I thought, but because of some encounters with other women, I tend to think that she was a person who was avoiding the pain of her life through snugly wrapping up in her blue blanket. And her blue blanket was constantly analyzing and reviewing her past, never doing anything about her painful memories, or taking any action, only examining what went wrong, why it went wrong, who was to blame. She seemed determined to spend life continually agonizing over her regrets and what ifs and if onlys.

Like that woman, we can use our catastrophic childhood or wretched past as a blue blanket to cover our heads and minds. That way, we don't have to get beyond the past and move on to what should be done now. We feel safe and snug hiding under this blue blanket.

It is occasionally and appropriately called "navel gazing." In this great escape hatch for dealing with yesterday's pain, we can endlessly review and reconstruct our past and find someone or something to blame for it all. This blue blanket can isolate us from people, relationships, and the world around us, sequestering us like a jury in deadlock, closing all the doors and windows of our lives and leaving us emotionally alienated and well on our way to living as lonely recluses.

We can take our cue from David to come from beneath this blue blanket. With this incredible past, which went from shepherding and flute playing, to king, adulterer, and murderer, David had every "reason" to hide beneath his blue blanket. Perhaps for a period of time he did, but when we read his words, "I have chosen the way of truth" (Ps. 119:30 KJV), we know that at some time or place David decided on an attitude change. He chose to move up and out of that hideous past and to lay aside the familiar comfort of this blue blanket. He gave himself freedom and permission to deal with the day's opportunities and challenges.

I am in no way suggesting that people with painful pasts can heal emotionally by simply "deciding" to have a positive attitude about it or that they should not talk about and deal with their pasts. However, when the talking becomes a rut instead of a bridge to recovery, the blue blanket of navel gazing takes control. If we are strong enough, we should make the choice to put down that blue blanket, move into the present and on to the future. If we've tried without success until we're practically hopeless, we should find professional help and trust God to use his "doctors" to turn our heart and face forward. Otherwise, the blue blanket of forever analyzing our past will only hold us more tightly in its grip.

Now, for my blue blanket: the one that is most difficult for me to nail down on paper.

THE BLUE BLANKET OF GOOD-BYE

Flying fully unfurled, yet held taut in the hurricane winds over the tallest cloud-covered pinnacles of my soul, used to be the flag of my blue blanket.

The flag represented heaven, the country I've always called home: that perpetually exquisite, glorified, and safe place; that wonderful place that is eternally free from death, war, hunger, poverty, brokenness, tears, loneliness, and pain-saturated nights.

I began fantasizing about heaven, this real but unseen country, when I was a little girl listening to my mother read aloud the classic story *The Pilgrim's Progress*. Established early in my mind was this story of Christian, who along with all of us, had begun a rather adventurous journey here on earth and was headed always in the general direction of our ultimate destination: heaven.

From hearing that story, I learned to believe as we walked the road of life it would at times be cold and snow clogged, hot and dusty, or filled with occasional steep inclines to traverse or cliffs to scale or crevices to jump over. I believed that perhaps the street pavement would be rough with potholes and sometimes a path or a bridge would be washed away by a flood. But all in all, nothing seriously harmful or bad could happen to us on our journey here to keep us out of heaven. After all, Christian made it; so will we. Even if death were to speed up the trip, that would only get us home sooner. Wasn't that our supreme goal?

My mother's enthusiasm for life gave me the optimistic courage of hope, and I felt sure that no matter how difficult the path, my journey would be a brief one—over like a flash of light or a snap of a finger and then, like Christian, I'd be home!

Good-bye, Earth!

Hello, Heaven!

However, on my way to heaven a funny thing happened. I grew up.

That nice little path of learning, that quiet tree-lined street of experience, and gently curving highway of life, love, and relationships were more like

no-exit alleys,

costly toll roads and bridges,

detours and alternate routes,

traffic snarled inner–city grid patterns,

fog- or ice-bound interstate highways, and

accidents on neighborhood streets or busy turnpikes

which crippled, maimed, or killed.

This kind of mental growing up and awareness to the heartsick pain of our journey knocks our childhood's naiveté and wonder straight out of us. Depression, situational or chronic, sets in; and given "significant losses," as the psychiatrists call them, we become prime candidates for the blue blanket of the "good-bye syndrome."

As I checked off my significant losses—death indiscriminately carrying off so many of my precious loved ones, the force of physical pain eroding and stripping away the last vestiges of energy and strength from me, and a pulverizing divorce, fragmenting and crushing what was left of my emotions—believe me, I was sick of the road. I was quite ready to trash my suitcase and never set foot outside my doorway again. "I'm not Christian, and this is not *Pilgrim's Progress*," I thought.

I began to visualize, both in my dreams at night and in

the clear light of day, the flag of my blue blanket. It grew more tempting by the hour to go home to heaven before something else dark and foreboding took place.

Emotionally and tentatively, I stretched out my hand toward the blue blanket of good-bye and I was amazed. I knew I didn't want to kill myself. There's nothing glamorous or reputable about suicide. Nor did I want to be an unnamed statistic. I just wanted to leave behind all the grief pain. I wanted to *get out!* I wanted God to call me home to him in heaven, quickly and accidentally, if at all possible.

In the early 1980s, when I touched my blue blanket, a surge of warm soothing anesthetic comfort would run through my whole system. It provided two words: *release* and *escape.* I easily embraced the blanket, and before I knew it, I was addicted. Soon I was like a little child again, never even thinking of going anywhere or spending a day without her blue blanket.

The well-documented statistics say that I'm not alone in clutching my blue blanket of good-bye. It is estimated that one out of ten people (that's 20 million Americans alone) suffer through debilitating episodes of chronic depression each year. And because of their significant losses, more than one million of those twenty million depressed souls will consider and reconsider suicide each year.

Years ago, I wrote of battling my depression and handling my suicidal tendencies. In my immature, gullible state of mind, I thought that depression, once licked stayed licked. Wrong. Unfortunately, unless we are in touch with our emotions and aware of our feelings, it's virtually impossible to assess the havoc that depression ushers into the soul of a person. More recently, I wrote about physical and emotional pain in *Silent September* (Austin, TX: Balcony). My insight about depression has significantly matured.

About the time I wrote *Silent September,* Keith Miller and I were collaborating on composing some songs for me to sing on a vocal album, *For People Who Don't Hear the Music Anymore.* I found understanding Keith's lyrics, especially "Short Cut Home," easy. His words exactly described my deepest heartfelt thoughts, and though the words *Blue Blanket* were not mentioned, Keith was sensitive and clearly heard my inner despair during our phone conversations. Later, he sent me the lyrics to "Short Cut Home." I put them to music and added a chorus. It goes like this:

SHORT CUT HOME

Remember when I was so young
So full of faith and coy,
The world all free from pain and doubt
A kaleidoscope of joy;
And then there came that little pain
The one I hardly knew,
An ache, a knife, and silent screams,
And now my life seems through.
I know I should not stop my days
Leave family and friends,
But something's snapped, the pain has won
So this must be the end;
I'm coming home to be with You
Or should I really try to stay?
Could You have meaning in such pain,
Oh God, I want to fly away.
I'm coming home to be with You.
There's nothing left to give,

Or can I live my pain for You
Dear Lord, I'll try to live;
So I guess I'll stay just one more day
And handle what time will bring,
I'll live my life and give again
But this one song I'll still sing.

Chorus

I wanna come home and be with You
dear Jesus,
I wanna come home and see Your face;
I wanna come home and be with You,
dear Jesus,
For I'm sick and tired of this lonely,
painful place.
I'm sick and tired of this place,
And I'm tired of the race
And I can't stand the pace
And I wanna come home
And be with you.[2]

The emotional pain and depression I was feeling was a few worlds beyond anything I'd experienced. I kept trying to find reasons for staying "one more day," as my daughter Laurie had said in *Silent September,* but my homesick feelings for heaven's shores only increased. There was hardly a moment that I did not frantically clutch my blue blanket and dream of how exquisite it would be to have the psalmist's "wings of a dove" and fly away home to be with God.

I'm afraid when I explained my feeling to family, close friends, or associates, very few could believe, understand, or take me seriously. I do not find fault with or blame them, but say this now because hindsight tells me this truth: Seldom can anyone fathom the mind of a person who actually begs and pleads with God to end their earthly journey. Unless, of course, they themselves have begged and pleaded.

Some people said I was just acting like a spoiled child to get my own way. Another group suggested that my ego wanted attention. Others ordered me to "snap out of it," and one pastor laughed when I told him I was suicidal as if I'd told him an amusing story he could use in the next Sunday morning service. Appallingly, a loved one and a few of my brothers and sisters in the faith suggested to me (and to others) that perhaps suicide was the answer. As they all agreed, "It would certainly settle things quickly and simplify the whole situation . . . and better than divorce."

This blue blanket may sound like today's newspaper. I've written nothing you don't already know. You were the people who, at my speaking engagements whispered in my ear or have written, "My blue blanket is the same as yours." Or maybe you're the woman who came to me after hearing my talk on *My Blue Blanket* and wept as she said, "My husband went out to the car but he asked me to tell you he's got the same blue blanket as you do. Would you remember him in prayer?"

We who are suffering from such depths of depression are not hell–bent on killing ourselves out of insanity or to get revenge or attention, nor do we have some superficial motive designed to make "someone sorry" for what they did to us. No, unfortunately this blue blanket is hugged tightly to our hearts and minds because we sincerely believe we have no more tolerance for life and its painful journey.

We who have been there, and are perhaps there right now, know the incredible and unthinkable truth of this woman's words when she wrote to me not long ago, "Every night I pray and ask the Lord to please not let me wake up *here* in the morning." Homeward to heaven simply becomes the Christian's national anthem, especially when it feels like every bone in our body is broken. Taking one more step feels impossible, and frantically, we long for this earthly journey to end.

"I'm calling Dr. Pannabecker," Francis informed me one morning. He had physically interfered with my attempt to self-destruct the previous night. After he had spent much of the night holding me in his arms as I mentally leaped back and forth over the dark chasm between living and dying, he decided to intervene and get me help.

One moment I'd calmly state, "I want to stay here with you, finish the journey, and carry out our mission statement as I believe God wants." The next instant, I'd plunge into the bottomless pit of depression and be on the edge of hysterics. Frantically, I'd say, "But I can't go on . . . I just can't . . . the pain of everything that has happened and that keeps on happening is too great to bear . . . there's no hope. I've no tolerance for these levels of intense pain." Then, I'd weep and whisper, "Good-bye, darling"—once more vaulting over the great chasm. Heaven was all I could think. If only I could be released . . . heaven.

When he arrived at our house, the tall, lanky doctor walked into our living room having heard only a brief synopsis from Francis about the depression that was oozing out of me. Immediately, he went straight to the heart of the matter. Before he sat down, he abruptly asked, "Joyce, why don't you stop running to your escape hatch?'' I hadn't the faintest idea of what he was talking about. "My what?"

Again he was direct. "Your escape hatch. Everyone has one but you can let go of it. So why don't you?"

My escape hatch was my instant desire to say good-bye and my desperate desire to go home to heaven and God. My escape hatch was the place to which I ran when the pain was too excruciating to endure any longer.

I sat down on our couch, stunned. All I could think was, *Stop running to my escape hatch? Give it up? My security blanket? My real source of comfort?* Here I was, teetering on the edge of sheer certifiable madness and quite capable of ending my life and this doctor was asking me to give up the thing that over the years had been my sane and soothing antidote to the insanity of my journey. *Is this man serious?*

He was, and as if he'd read my thoughts, Dr. Pannabecker, with a sense of quiet urgency, began laying out several important concepts for me. Perhaps you will find them important (even appropriate) for you too.

"Joyce, perhaps it feels easier for you to deal with being dead rather than having to deal with the pain of being alive, or the realities of life and what needs to be done in your life." They were stone and steel words, hard to hear, but they were so kindly spoken and rang with such truth I was compelled to listen. He went on.

"If you let go of your escape hatch, it's almost a paradox. For at the point of letting go, your energy is available to deal with the problem rather than always being used to run away from the conflict." He paused. He riveted his attention on me while waiting for my answer. When I remained silent, Dr. Pannabecker probed again, "Why don't you give up your escape hatch?"

"I'll have to think about it," I finally said. "I'll give you an answer when I can."

It was a feeble reply on my part, I'll admit, but I had the feeling that somehow the good doctor had handed me the opportunity to catch a wild tiger by its tail and then, against all odds, tame it. But I wasn't sure I wanted to catch the tiger, much less tame it.

During the two weeks that followed our first session, I began peeling back the layers of my soul. Desperately, I wanted truth to emerge, but I found I didn't want to give up my escape hatch. I didn't want to let go of my special friend, my blue blanket. I spent a good deal of that time prying under the layers of my soul, trying to find out why I couldn't or wouldn't let go of my blanket.

I reasoned that when I held tightly to my blue blanket I didn't have to face any conflicts or take any responsibility for them. That felt good. I didn't have to deal with any ugliness in people, demolished relationships, or failed situations. That felt good. I didn't even have to forgive or pray for any of my enemies. That felt wonderful. I could just disappear into the folds of my blue blanket and fade away. Frankly, when I wrapped my battle-scarred self in such a nurturing and healing blanket, it gave large measures of comfort and relief to my soul. Or was I just deluding myself about the whole thing?

Each time I came close to the decision place of hanging on to or letting go of my blue blanket, the war within me would rage on anew. Then my mind's eye would see Dr. Pannabecker and I'd hear him calmly asking, "Why don't you stop running to it?"

Slowly, I started contemplating what my life might be like if, when pain overwhelmed me and threatened to annihilate my sanity, I let go of my blanket. What if I folded it up out of my mind and heart and set it aside?

Those thoughts frightened me at first. They deeply disturbed and threatened my security. I could scarcely imagine not running to my escape hatch or not hugging my blue blanket of good-bye. But scarier still was the thought that if my journey got any rougher (as I knew it probably would) I could end up wasting a formidable amount of my life's energy forever. I could spend the rest of my time on earth running away from conflicts instead of dealing with them. I could hug the blue blanket until I really did take my life or until God chose to call me home, whichever happened first. But I had to ask myself was that really what, in my heart of hearts, I wanted to do?

Remember, I said earlier that blue blankets are not necessarily harmful in and of themselves but when a blue blanket is abusive and dangerous to one's health, or ruins and destroys other people, then it is very deadly. That is when the blanket, not you, is controlling your life.

I knew my blue blanket was the deadly type, and I decided I didn't want this beloved blue blanket of mine to own me. I had to face the fact that I wasn't an innocent two year old with an equally innocent blue blanket, just wanting the simple security and the warm feelings it gave the little boy in the grocery store. I also understood that I needed a radical attitude change if I was ever going to be in control of my life instead of that blanket.

On the third session we had with Dr. Pannabecker, I told him I was letting go. I was willing to stop running to my escape hatch. I would lay aside my blue blanket. It had to go.

Mentally, I took my tattered, faded, and much-loved blue blanket out of the living room of my life. I folded it up and tucked it away on the top shelf in the closet. I know it's there, but my heart and spirit are a lot healthier now that I have deliberately chosen to put my blue blanket away. I am not a child. I am a responsible adult, dealing, head on, with the pain of reality as I see what needs to be done in my life.

Dr. Pannabecker was right, it was easier to deal with the idea of my being dead and in heaven than with that of my staying alive and trying to work things out. I've always been more comfortable running away from pain than standing bravely in the gap.

Not too long after these painful yet life-giving sessions, an opportunity was presented to me which ordinarily would have sent my panic-stricken heart into a tailspin of depression. Usually, I would have frantically reached for my blue blanket and my bottle of saved-up pills, but I stopped midway to the closet and asked myself if hugging my blanket and retreating to the dark places behind my soul was what I really wanted.

No, I think not. Definitely not.

The journey here on earth seems to get more dangerous with the years and there are no shortcuts home. But in reading and pondering Dr. Viktor Frankl's question to the survivors of Auschwitz concentration camp, "Why *didn't* you take your life in the death camp?" I've taken a different view of these traveling days and my old blue blanket.

Those 1940s death camp survivors who turned away from starving themselves or decided against running into the wall so they'd be shot chose another way. They looked for and found one thread, one slender thread that bound them to keep living rather than giving in to dying. Some chose to stay one more day because there was a child living safely outside of Nazi Germany that they wanted to see once more. One man was a medical doctor and a scholar who had written eleven books of a twelve-book series before his internment and he wanted to live to go home and finish the series. Others had different reasons, but they chose to live, even at Auschwitz. They put away their blue blankets of good-bye because the threads of unfinished business, slim as they might have been, kept their sense of self-preservation alive.

The threads which keep my blue blanket put away in the closet are very real and precious to me, even on the days (like a few weeks ago) when we were at a Christian radio station. I was stunned by the sharp pain of an unexpected encounter with a couple of individuals who did their best to wound me into believing I should leave the field of Christian writing.

Hours later when I was crying into Francis' shoulder, I found myself saying, "It's really okay. I'll be all right, darling, but do you mind if I tell you that I feel like opening the closet door and just looking at my blue blanket for a little bit?" As I said before, I've chosen (and it was not a quick simplistic decision to make) to fold up my blue blanket and put it away in the closet. I've got too many threads to ignore, too many precious reasons for staying, too many hurting people in crisis needing recovery and too many things crying out to be finished before I leave and go home.

If you stood face to face with me right now and you said you were at the end of your rope, and unless something extraordinary happened or some miracle of God took place that you were grabbing your blue blanket of good-bye and leaving, I'd tell you these three things:

1. I believe you. I understand your despair and I don't question your motives nor blame you for your thoughts or your actions. I love you and I wait with you.

2. I'd urge you to look around you to find one thread, no matter how slim or fragile, that calls out begging for you to stay your hand. Look for one thread that provides you with the energy to continue your journey, to endure and to press on no matter how difficult or insane that may seem.

3. I'd ask you the same question Dr. Pannabecker asked me, "Why don't you stop running to your escape hatch?" Why not choose to fold up your blanket, lay it aside on the top shelf of the closet and shut the door? Why not?

No matter what our blue blanket may be—sleeping, eating, reading, telephoning, watching TV, movies, busyness, alcohol, drugs, pills, analyzing the past, saying good-bye, or some private unnamed blanket—no matter how safe or how lethal it is, no matter what intensity of addiction it has for you, and no matter whether it's real or perceived, it's not too late to put away that blue blanket.

I pray that these brief words will help you to choose, as arduous and rough as it may be, to lay aside and let go of your blue blanket, especially the blanket which may set up the standards for your life, which may enslave your heart and mind, and which may deplete your reserves of mental, emotional, and spiritual energy leaving you too exhausted, too hopeless, and too despairing to press on with your journey.

And one last word before I close this chapter: I am

choosing to trust God for all of us that he will be our beautiful blanket of comfort for today and for all our tomorrows here on earth before we see him face to face at journey's end.

In his time, God really does make all things beautiful, especially our decision to lay aside our blue blankets, to get up to hold on to that slender thread, walk the path, to carry the cross, and to continue the journey.

FIVE

I CHOOSE TO BE A WOUNDED HEALER

We were waiting for a sales clerk to ring up our purchases at the counter. It was nearly closing time at Dillard's department store in Austin, Texas, and very nearly Christmastime for the whole country. Finally, Francis left to go browsing through some racks of men's suits and slacks and as I waited, I leaned wearily against the counter. It had been one of those unusually long days filled with the typical pre-Christmas stress and foreboding.

Impatient and bored, I put an old habit into my mental computer and I began studying the salesman as he finished with the customers ahead of me. Our friend, and author, Pastor John Hagee, once told me the difference between readers and writers was that "readers see words and writers see people." So I watched the clerk's

eyes and face and tried to hear what his tone of voice was
really saying as he talked to the people beside me.

Then it was my turn, but just as the clerk asked, "May I
help you?" he stopped and winced slightly. Obviously in
pain he pressed his hand over his abdomen.

"Are you all right?"

"Sure" he said matter-of-factly reaching for the items
in my hand. I held them back and tried to get him to
look me in the eye. Leaning toward him, I said, "I'm
really asking, are you all right?"

On the spot, he decided I was not greeting him but
asking him, so he looked at me and, in a very tired voice,
gave me a recital about his ulcer which was kicking up
again. Launching into a sad inventory about his temporary Christmas employment schedule, he said, "Sales
work is demanding you know, and they give us only a
short break for lunch." He rambled on.

As I stood there listening to this doleful litany, I wanted
to have a long mother-to-son talk with him about his
attitude. I wanted to emphasize that given the financially
grievous conditions of the Texas economy, he should be
grateful to have a job. To have even a temporary job was
better than no job at all. I wanted to tell him that if he'd
decide to change his attitude he'd probably enjoy working a tad more and his ulcer might even settle down. I
wanted to encourage him to do the very best job he
could (no one would ask more than that) and to let the
rest do just that: rest. I wanted to tell him those things.

Instead, I told him truthfully how terribly sorry I was
that he was having ulcer pain. I said I wished that the
pain would go away and gently reminded him that the
season would be over in a few more shopping days. Then
I said, "I'll pray that your ulcer pain calms down." At

this the dour salesman smiled, straightened up his shoulders a bit and allowed, "Oh, I think I'll make it. I'll be all right . . . at least, I've got my Maalox!" We both laughed. I know about Maalox™.

Our transactions completed, Francis and I left the men's department amid the salesman's cheerily shouting his best wishes for our merriest of Christmases. As we walked away, I began to relate to my husband the details of my encounter. I told him what I felt like telling the salesman (but hadn't) and what I actually did say. When I finished, Francis stopped in the middle of the aisle just as we were leaving the store and commented, "The man just wanted some comfort."

How true. Don't we all?

I had "felt led" to give the man verbal instructions and solutions for getting through the Christmas rush. And as I told Francis, I'd had a mind to give him some well-chosen advice about his apparent lack of gratitude for the sales job he was able to hold down, and I'd also had a hankering to pontificate on the value of positive thinking.

But Francis was right. All the man really needed was comfort. I doubt he wanted pity or sympathy. He, like most of us do from time to time, wanted another human being to be understanding and to give him some level of comfort.

Driving home that night, I kept wondering what it was about the clerk that I sensed or saw which made me forget my admonitions and sermonettes? Whatever it was, I found myself, instead of giving him what I thought he needed, almost inadvertently giving him small measures of comfort. But as I turned over the whole sequence in my mind, it became obvious. I realized that when I looked into the man's face as he winced because of his ulcer pain, I saw my own pain reflected in his eyes, and instantly I felt a sharp twinge of that *remembered* pain.

When I watched the way the salesman's shoulders drooped and saw the lines around his mouth that sagged and turned downward, I saw my own body language of weary despair. Seeing this man and my own reflected image as well, feeling his pain and being able to relate to his exhaustion, I found myself unable to sermonize, inept at lecturing and incapable of giving solutions. I thought about what I'd want if I were the clerk and he were the customer. When I looked at him through those lenses, it was fairly easy to hug him with words, to assure him I understood his feelings, to verbally wish that his pain would ease or go away and to give him hope that God would carry him through the "tis-the-season-to-be-jolly" time.

I may never have found a psychological or spiritual explanation or a name for my Good-Samaritan rush into giving a stranger some comfort that night had it not been for a small book Francis bought for me in February, two months after that encounter at Dillard's.

The Dutch priest Henri J. M. Nouwen has contributed greatly to our head and heart knowledge about God and about our relationships to him and to our fellow mankind. But in this particular volume, written basically as a handbook to help ministers really minister, Nouwen, as he does so well, takes serving and ministering to others beyond the established pastor. And as the pages unfolded, I could easily see that he felt everyone, all the people, not just the ministers, was called to the work of serving and ministering and healing. Nouwen didn't exclude any of us who are without a degree in theology.

Instead, he gave us all a wonderful hallmark phrase for the comfort and healing that takes place when one human being, recognizing the suffering of another, reaches out to that hurting person because he has suffered the same pain.

To all of us who would serve God, yet who are hurting from all kinds of devastating traumas, Henri Nouwen gives us a name: Wounded Healers. And that phrase has caught up my heart in an awesome way.

In the introduction of *The Wounded Healer,* Nouwen wrote:

> For the minister is called to recognize the sufferings of his time in his own heart and make that recognition the starting point of his service. Whether he tries to enter into a dislocated world, relate to a convulsive generation, or speak to a dying man, his service will not be perceived as authentic unless it comes from a heart wounded by the suffering about which he speaks.
>
> Thus nothing can be written about ministering without a deeper understanding of the ways in which the minister can make his own wounds available as a source of healing.[1]

In my own life, and in the lives of my loved ones, I want to see and find some meaning in the pain of suffering. "Making our own wounds available as a source of healing," being able to comfort and heal others, is the first step which makes sense of these horrible wounds and turns them into something of meaning and purpose.

How do we turn the suffering of our own life into

comfort and healing for others? And what exactly are wounded healers?

Out of the fiction of my imagination, and the truth of my "layman's" knowledge, research and personal experiences, let me see if I can paint a present-day portrait of a *medical* wounded healer before I write about an *emotional* wounded healer. Come on, pretend with me.

Say over an extended period of time, you're talking with a friend of yours who has multiple sclerosis. She mentions that many of her problems "looked like" symptoms of other diseases and that it took her doctors a long time to sort them all out and to finally give her the correct diagnosis. This little bit of information strikes you as interesting. Your friend's comment about the "looked-like" symptoms being hard to sort out echoes in your mind and takes a hold of you. You're not sure why; it just does.

What you do know is that for months now your own body has been giving you some alarming messages. You think something is wrong. No, it's not; yes, it is, your mind goes. Armed with your friend's words, you go to see your doctor. You tell him about your friend and he admits that sometimes symptoms do look like, cover, or mask the real problem. He also admits that your joint inflammation may well be rheumatoid arthritis or the joint pain could be masking another disease altogether. Then, looking at your charts, he begins to connect your history with pleurisy and anemia and after a moment says, "Maybe we ought to look in a different direction."

Somehow you feel a small puzzle piece has just slipped into place.

Your doctor schedules you for an LE Prep. That microscopic test of your blood preparation plops another puzzle piece adroitly into position because this time your doctor tells you he suspects you may be suffering from a disease called lupus. He recommends a specialist.

Later that week, as you sit in the waiting room of the "he-comes-highly-recommended" doctor's office, you find yourself edgy, even a little skeptical about all doctors, highly recommended or not. You've had a few years of seeing doctors, including your own family doctor and now they "think" you may have lupus, so here you sit waiting for a lupus specialist so he can tell you what? You're pretty convinced that all he can really do is affirm what you've known for a long time now, that there is something very wrong with you.

When you get your first glimpse of this specialist, your skepticism grows considerably. You even wonder if there's been a mistake. He looks too young to be a doctor. He resembles your eighteen-year-old kid brother and you wonder what he could possibly know about medicine in general or lupus specifically.

His physical examination is professional, thorough and brief. He says little but asks a number of questions and then grows quiet as he studies your medical records and test results.

When the examination is over, you get dressed and a nurse leads you into the doctor's office to wait for him. Again, as you see him, you are confused by his youthful appearance. But before he's spoken a few sentences or two, something tells you that this doctor is different. Very different. This young man, for some reason strikes you not as just a doctor, but as a physician, a born healer. You feel within seconds that this doctor knows everything about you.

He begins by talking in low and measured tones about your test results and what information he has discovered from his physical examination. He quietly verifies that you do have lupus. He goes on to say, "There are two kinds of lupus. Discoid lupus which is a chronic disease of the skin and the other called Systemic Lupus Erythematosus (SLE), which is a deep-seated disease, especially if the vital organs are involved, such as the kidneys. "Systemic Lupus," he says in a quiet measured tone, "can be fatal."

His eyes never leave your face as he hesitantly pronounces with obvious sadness, "Your lupus is systemic."

While you are trying to assimilate the ramifications of the words you've just heard, the doctor gets up, comes around his desk and sits in a chair beside you. And then, as if he's had a secret microscope or a giant magnifying glass focused on your whole life, he quietly details exactly what you are feeling in your emotions and what your thought process is at this moment. He is surprisingly accurate.

When you begin to realize the doctor is describing in very precise detail your mental, physical and emotional state, it stuns you. You are accustomed to telling and retelling doctors your symptoms, including how you feel, where the pain is and what happens to you emotionally and physically, not them telling you! You can hardly believe how right on the doctor's words are.

In his quiet, yet perceptive direct way, this boyish looking man, sits there and tells you every symptom you've ever experienced. He perfectly describes how you feel when your joints ache. He discusses the reddish skin rash you often have and how you feel when the red patches spread across your cheeks and the bridge of your nose, somewhat resembling a butterfly with open wings. He speaks with equal ease and compassion about some of the odd, somewhat ridiculous, even weird symptoms you have: how every hair on your head and over your body "hurts" and that you sometimes have the strange sensation that your "teeth itch."

You feel numb in hearing the name of the disease which has plagued you with pain. But you also feel relief in knowing its name and finding what exactly is wrong. One moment you have a thousand questions; the next, none come to mind. But you are astonished over the doctor's complete grasp and knowledge of how painful your symptoms are, as well as his diagnosis.

In the past you'd eventually refused to relate the bizarre details about your hair and teeth symptoms because of other doctors' raised, questioning eyebrows, their patronizing pats on your head, as if you'd crossed the border between real and what you've imagined to be real, and their declarations that "hair hurting" and "teeth itching" were merely your mind's products of your psychosomatic disease. Yet here sits this doctor taking you and your lupus seriously, even believing your wild symptoms, as well as your test results, and never minimizing your unbearable pain for one instant.

The doctor finishes presenting each facet of your physical, emotional and mental existence and pledges to try every alternative, promising to run down every medical lead, and ends by telling you he is with you and will see you through this. Your brain and heart are racing.

"But doctor, how do you know so much about me and my pain? How do you know?"

"Because," he measures his words carefully, "because, I have the same disease."

You lean forward and whisper, "Systemic lupus, like mine?"

He nods his head, "Yeah."

Though this doctor is a product of my mind, he is, nevertheless, a world-class example of what it takes to be a great wounded healer.

When his lupus is diagnosed he does not choose to throw in the towel, give up in despair or become embittered over all the time and money spent in med school. No, he deliberately chooses to go on, to continue his practice. He chooses the attitude of healing. He reaches out to others who suffer from lupus, and in doing so he becomes a wounded healer.

There are millions of us who can choose to be wounded healers. We can minister, serve and help hurting people in God's name and be effective beyond belief because we have or are suffering from their same diseases or we have had or are having a wounding experience which has helped us to expand our vision toward other suffering souls.

Wounded healers don't choose their specific mission in life. Certainly they don't choose to be wounded. And wounded healers don't become crushed and shattered accidentally or by some odd collection of extenuating circumstances.

Wounded healers are chosen by God and born out of God's design coupled with the winepress of life itself. Being a wounded healer starts with a God-calling as the writer of Hebrews points out concerning the criteria for the Jewish high priest:

And because he is a man he can deal gently with other men, though they are foolish and ignorant, for he, too, is surrounded with the same temptations and understands their problems very well (Heb. 5:2 LB).

J. B. Phillips translates this same passage of scripture by saying of the high priest:

He must be able to deal sympathetically with the ignorant and foolish because he realizes that he is himself prone to human weakness.

Look at this same passage as it is in the Amplified Bible:

He is able to exercise gentleness and forbearance toward the ignorant and erring, since he himself also is liable to moral weakness and physical infirmity. And because of this he is obliged to offer sacrifice for his own sins as well as for those of the people.

This is followed immediately by:

Another thing to remember is that no one can be a high priest [a wounded healer] *just because he wants to be. He has to be called by God for this work in the same way God chose Aaron* (Heb. 5:4 LB).

Wounded healers are called of God and though they take no delight in being wounded and would just as soon avoid the intensity of the pain, whether it's physical, mental or emotional, they deliberately choose to accept their God-calling. True wounded healers are the people who, though grievously wounded, sometimes to the extreme of dying, instead of giving up with the burden and onslaught of lonely despair, unbearable pain and a deep sense of hopelessness choose to use their knowledge and experience as a gift from God to comfort. They choose to reach out with healing hands to others with similar wounds, admitting their own pain and, as Henri Nouwen wrote, giving them a deeper understanding of the ways one can make his own wounds available as a source of healing.

> *True wounded healers are the people who . . . choose to use their knowledge and experience as a gift from God to comfort.*

When we come dead center, face to face with the reality of our own lives, we must deal with probably one of the most important choices of our lives. We must ask ourselves if we'll accept the wounding process as our *God-calling,* our gift that qualifies us to reach out to comfort and to heal others or if we will choose, because of the pain of our hemorrhaging wounds, to isolate ourselves from others, to crawl in some dark hole, licking the bitter gall of our losses, and never again to trust God or his people. If we do the latter, we will spend the rest of our days on earth in the company of a three-headed monster named Fear, Resentment and Loneliness.

I pray, dear wounded friend, for both of us that we will

recognize these hideous bruising and battering experiences of ours for a purpose far higher and greater. For I believe we are called of God in a very unique way to grasp the momentous opportunity we have been handed on such a rugged platter. We have the chance, should we choose to take it, to use our wounds as our earned credentials for the incredible compassionate work of a wounded healer. In effect, our work to serve and minister is that of a high priest, called of God. And we are reminded by him who knows all about the wounding process to deal gently and with understanding in the lives of other wounded souls.

What better thing could be accomplished out of the awfulness of life's unfair, unjust, unworld ways? What good can come from our hard and painful "credentials" if it is not found in comforting those with similar diseases? Is there a better idea or way to give any semblance of meaning to our suffering? I doubt it. Furthermore, I don't believe God gives us this unique gift purely for our own growth and learning curve, but also to send healing and growth into the lives of others.

Often when I've told someone my painful and unreal symptoms, they've lightly tossed back to me comments about God's teaching me something. Here's a mega clue: When someone glibly pats you on the back after you've been vulnerable enough to share your pain and they tell you it's for your own good or growth, beware. You are not in a safe country. Take the next train out.

Of course it's a truism that everything that happens to us presents us with some sort of learning experience and chance for growth. But we must exercise a little caution in who we listen to and in our choice of "high priests." Not all "high priests" are wounded healers.

When we are in terrible pain and cry out to others, some people, even some professionals (counselors, pastors, doctors) are not yet wounded healers. They may be someday, but as of now they haven't walked through their own valley of suffering or loss, and God has not yet called them to come to the wounding place. So they may listen to us as we describe the pain, but their first words sometimes are brittle, "learned behavior" responses. They utter words which sometimes come from ignorance of pain or a denial of their pain or out of someone else's training or teaching. But, definitely, their response is not out of their own valley of suffering. Their words do not touch us with comfort and healing. It's as if we are listening to an executive giving a medical lecture in an office conference room rather than watching a doctor binding up wounds in a hospital.

The effective, called-of-God wounded healers speak to the hurting with real words, because they are very sensitive and well acquainted with their own pain.

We don't even come close to being wounded healers when we respond to the physically and emotionally sick and dying around us by pointing out their need for "learning and growth." And we are definitely not wounded healers when, after we've heard the details of another's pain we offer up one or several of these shattering, crushing statements:

"I'm shocked and disappointed in you."

"I think you should have been more obedient and responsible."

"I fear you have made a big mistake."

"I can't understand why you were so stupid, careless, naive."

"My son would never take drugs or be a homosexual."

"My teenaged daughter would never get pregnant."

"I always knew you'd end up like this."

"You must have done something bad to have your kids turn out that way."

"Thank God, I'd never be guilty of that."

"I haven't called or been with you because people might think I'm condoning your decision, actions, lifestyle. I want to avoid the appearance of evil."

"I haven't seen any remorse or repentance on your face or in your life."

"You're lying about the sexual abuse of your childhood."

If these are our "learned behavior" responses to the walking wounded around us, then it's probably safe to assume that the only wounding that has taken place in our lives was very slight and our mind has silently erased the pain and the memory of it. We will be ineffective, unable to serve and minister, possibly even doing damage to the hurting people in the world around us. We haven't had the wounding experience, hence there is no call as yet to serve as a wounded healer. A healer? Perhaps yes, but not a wounded healer.

I can't speak or write for your heartfelt desires or mind's intent, but I feel certain in my desire to be what God wants me to be (faithful to my mission statement). And I really don't want to be anything but a wounded healer. What greater growth and deeper learning can come out of our broken, crushed and pain-ravaged hearts and minds if it's not in becoming a wounded healer to others?

As I've recalled the people who have suffered much and become wonderful wounded healers in my own life, they are people who, almost with one voice, have said yes to their special calling. They've chosen to reach out to others in the name and love of Jesus Christ. They seem to always know how to give us comfort without criticism, to bring us joy instead of judgments and perhaps best of all, to provide grace to us without tacking on a pound or two of guilt.

Apparently, wounded healers look at others through the eyes of careful reality for they seem to be able to find and identify the hurting people around them. They seem good at reviewing their own diseases, their own pinpricks of remembered pain, and what comes out of their hearts invariably is healing. These healers are like my fictitious doctor and his lupus patient when he says, "I know about your pain because I suffer from the same disease."

Wounded healers, whether their disease is exactly like ours or not, are the world's best listeners. They hear beyond the spoken words, they see beyond the tears, and they read the hidden messages of the heart. They relate, even feel, the burning, stinging pain within us. So when we finish our story and dry our tears, they say things like this: "I hear your heart. I cannot change the ugly circumstances of your life or pull out the dagger in your soul, but I can see you and hear you clearly. I know about suffering, maybe not the particulars of your suffering. But from the pain I've had, I know that pain is pain is pain is pain."

Each December thirty-first, my grief pain for my infant son, David, who died the afternoon of the day he was born always rises up and engulfs me. This year though, when I was experiencing that profound sadness a mother feels when her child goes on before her, my wounded healer husband rescued my sinking heart.

Francis came in our kitchen door with an envelope in his hands marked "To a dear Mother of three." He sat me down, lit a small votive candle in a china holder he'd just bought and waited as I opened the envelope. Inside was a card with a photograph covering the whole front of the card. For a moment it took my breath away. The photograph was a close-up of a baby's face, precious and beautiful, a blue-eyed baby looking much like I remembered David looking in my fleeting glance at him seconds after he was born.

When I opened the card, Francis had written:

Darling,

> My heart has never felt the depths of grief for the death of a son. But for you, dear Mother of David, my heart reaches out at least to try to ease the pain of those memories.

He and I adore you!!!

My husband, a true wounded healer, even though he has not lost his son, has through the death of his dearly beloved brother, endured his own painful losses, and his own God-calling has well equipped him to give compassionate and comforting healing touches to those who are hurting, including me.

This same weekend I was also touched by a friend who has endured much wounding and has suffered many tragic losses. I've never met her except through our correspondence. And I doubt she knows David died the last day of December, yet she wrote:

> Don't know if this is a "my own concern" or the prompting of the Holy Spirit, but I'm writing you

to let you know I'm holding you in prayer most
especially tonight.

I know I don't know what is wrong, but while
praying for you in the Spirit just now, I was overcome by tears of pain for you, and feeling pain in
my heart for you. I felt led to uphold both you and
Doc [Francis].

I want you to be comforted in assuring you, that
the Holy Spirit is with you to comfort you and
guide you right now in whatever you're going
through, and that God sends you His love and
peace which transcends all understanding.

Her letter went on to give me comfort with several
passages of scripture from Isaiah and the Psalms. This
friend is a wounded healer; even though she's not suffered the loss of a child, she is struggling with her own
painful diseases. How grateful I am that she heard the
Lord and wrote those dear words. It was as if God was
sending his message of love to my heart, to her heart and
back again to mine.

Francis and others, because of their own dreadful
woundings, have brought me to a new place in my grief
this year over my long lost little baby David. In ministering to me and giving their assurances of love, they freed
me to lay out and handle some long denied parts of my
unresolved grief. Their comfort and healing words told
me it was all right for me to grieve over David's death
and equally all right for me to still miss him.

I thank God for obedient wounded healers who are
sensitive and who are listening to the gentle prompting
of the Holy Spirit when one sister or brother is
hurting.

I think the wounded healer concept is what Paul had

in mind when he was training and teaching the people of the early Church in the practical ways of dealing with life and each other.

When the people in the church at Corinth were suffering in some of the same ways we suffer these days—with broken dreams, broken relationships, broken hearts, broken spirits, broken health and broken promises— they must have voiced their questions and concerns to Paul. It's possible they, like us, wondered what earthly good or purpose pain and brokenness could possibly accomplish in their lives. But Paul, already having suffered much and having heard his God-calling, answered them with truths I believe he had experienced firsthand.

He wrote to them that our great God "comforts us and strengthens us in our hardships and trials" as if he were laying out a pattern for us to follow. Paul asks the Corinthians, "Why does he do this?" Then he answers his own question: "So that when others are troubled, needing our sympathy and encouragement, we can pass on to them this same help and comfort God has given us" (2 Cor. 1:3,4 LB).

A woman wrote me a letter regarding this scripture. She described the unreal pain of her own experiences and then wrote:

Second Corinthians 1:3 and 4 was the spiritual and emotional core that kept me hobbling through the valley of rejection. Today I use it as a reminder to myself to seek out others whose emotions are ravaged.

Wounded healers know the pain of the wounding process and they accept their God-calling as a gift. They are very sensitive and aware of God's bringing them comfort and strength through others. So in turn, they become wounded healers watching for and "seeking out" those wounded souls who litter the battlefields of life.

Wounded healers, also like my fictional doctor, often describe our symptoms and understand them before we have a chance to spell everything out. Wounded healers say things like:

"I know you can't believe the horror of what's happening right now, but I do. I'll wait with you so you won't be alone during this terrible storm."

"I know you can't think or pray right now, but I can. I'll lift you up before God's throne each day until you can pray once more."

"I know you can't read the scriptures right now, but I can. I'll read the great promises and they will speak of love and grace to ease your aching heart."

"I know you can't trust anyone right now, but I can. I'll trust our heavenly Father to give you his strength and his power, his peace and his rest for your weary heart."

"I know you think you won't stop bleeding, your broken soul won't mend and there's no hope of your recovering right now, but I can believe for you. I'll be, as someone described it, 'God with skin on' to you. I'll not judge or condemn you, for I remember that we Christians are called to serve and heal, not to judge or control. I'll bind up your wounds as best I can and with God's help I'll hug you back to life again."

"Believe me, it's all right that for now, because you are too shattered, too vulnerable and too wounded, you can't hear the music. But I can. I'll sing for you until you begin to sing again."

"I know all this about you, dear hurting person, because I suffer from the same disease."

The song on my vocal album that really sums up these wounded healer phrases best is " 'Til You Hear the Music." The lyrics are written by Claire Cloninger and the perfect music by Jeff Kennedy. I wish I could sing it for you right now, but since I can't, here are Claire's words:

'TIL YOU HEAR THE MUSIC

Somewhere in the silence
There's a song that you once heard,
Playing softly at a distance
But you just can't hear the words;
And my heart is aching for you
'Cause I've known your pain before
And I've been one of the people
Who don't hear the music anymore.

But now I'll be the song for you
I'll be the symphony
'Til you feel the harmony.
From deep within
I'll bring His words;
And sing His melody
'Til you hear the music once again,
'Til you hear the music once again.

Let me stand against your silence
Let me touch you with His song,
Just believe me it's still playing
For I hear it loud and strong,
When the still of night has broken
There's a morning song, I'm sure,
For I've been one of the people
Who don't hear the music anymore.

And when the morning wakes you
You'll hear it all so clear,

And you'll be the one that's singing
For those who cannot hear.

Yes you'll be the song for them
You'll be the symphony
'Til they feel the harmony
From deep within;
You'll bring His words
And sing His melody
'Til they hear the music once again,
'Til they hear the music once again.[2]

Wounded healers, because they know their own pain,
become our singer of songs until we are strong enough
to hear the music too so that we can sing "once more."

In the late eighteen hundreds, almost seventy years
before the discovery of the sulfur drug, a leper colony
was established on the Kalaupapa peninsula of the island
of Molokai in the South Pacific. There, a thirty-three-
year-old Belgian priest volunteered to serve. It was to be
a "temporary mission," but the priest, Father Damien
Joseph de Veustec, felt he had been chosen by "Divine
Providence" (his God-calling) to stay. So he stayed to
serve the mutilated and forsaken lepers.

When Robert Louis Stevenson wrote about this leper
colony in *Travels in Hawaii*, his description of the lepers
themselves gave us probably a very accurate picture of
the lepers Father Damien saw when he reached his par-
ish. Stevenson wrote:

They were strangers to each other,
Collected by common calamity, disfigured,
mortally sick, banished without sin
from home and friends. Few would
understand the principle on which they
were thus forfeited in all that makes

life dear; many must have conceived their
ostracism to be grounded in malevolent
caprice; all came with sorrow at heart,
many with despair and rage.[3]

Father Damien lived among the lepers for the rest of
his life, not only performing his priestly duties at St.
Philomena Church but also changing the lepers' dress-
ings, bandaging their sores, building coffins, houses and
chapels, and engineering a water system for them.

Twelve years after he arrived, at the age of forty-five,
Father Damien himself became a leper. He wrote that
year: "I hope to be eternally thankful to God for this
favor as it seems to me that this disease may shorten a
little, and even make more direct, my road."[4]

Before he died four years later in 1889, this specially
gifted wounded healer who called the disease of leprosy
a "favor," brought the desperate plight of lepers to the
world's attention. He spent his last days caring for and
comforting his beloved friends, the lepers.

Perhaps you and I may not be a glorious or renowned
wounded healer like Father Damien, but still we can
choose to use our pain. We can take inventory of all our
unworld experiences, all the physical and emotional pain
we've suffered and survived and choose to use it to be a
wounded healer to others.

I think I've been a wounded healer for years now,
without really naming it. But now I am deliberately
choosing to take the things which have hurt me the most
and use them to be the wounded healer I should be. I
am deliberately choosing to look at the pain of my diseases as my God-calling and my credentials, and I am
deliberately choosing to reach out to others using my

knowledge of pain to bring healing to others who share a common disease.

At a speaking engagement last year I was talking about being a wounded healer. Just as I was at this point about using our hurts to help heal others, I couldn't help noticing a woman in the audience who was about my age. She was sitting on the aisle, three rows from the front, and was in obvious distress. Her head was bowed and her shoulders were shaking from the intensity of her sobbing.

She was the first one to reach me when I concluded this "Blue Blanket" talk. Usually my brain is "fried mush" following a speaking engagement, but somehow I was not too emotionally drained or too physically exhausted to catch the import of her words. Her story, as nearly as I can remember it, was the stuff movie writers thrive on.

She had been arrested, tried, convicted, and sentenced for fraud. She was accused of embezzling funds from her office. All through the trial she declared her innocence, but the jury was convinced otherwise and they brought in the verdict of guilty. She was sent to the women's state prison to serve her time.

She told me a little of the horrors of prison life, including how bitterly angry she had become with everyone, including God. She'd lost everything and everyone.

Then one year ago, after serving seven years of her sentence, the real embezzler was caught. The woman was released from prison and given a full pardon. But she told me that ever since her release she'd been unable to find any peace of mind. She had no feeling of freedom. She could not understand the reason for seven long lost and wasted years. She kept asking why and what was the point of it all? What was she supposed to have learned? Where was God when she needed him and why was he so silent for those seven years? She was a Christian before she went to prison, but upon being released she was disillusioned with God, suffering bitter pain and loneliness at having lost everyone and everything.

Then she told me that as she had listened to the wounded healer concept, she'd heard her very own specific God-calling. She had wept because suddenly seven years of prison, seven years of horrific wounding, had handed her an earned doctorate in being a wounded healer. Before my talk had ended, the woman had decided she would go back to the same prison she'd served time in and be a wounded healer to those still inside.

"I can tell them I know how they feel!" she exclaimed. "I know how they hurt and I can be a wounded healer to them. I know this because I've suffered from the same disease!" We wept together.

* * *

. . . when we take the pain that comes very close to killing us and begin to use it to reach out to others . . . What a ministry we have!

* * *

If I could look into your eyes, stand face to face with you, I'd ask these questions: "Where do you hurt the most?" "Where is the main viscera of your greatest injury, physical, mental, emotional or spiritual?"

Whenever we can identify and articulate our most awful hurts, we can choose which way we'll go concerning our attitudes and how we will deal with the pain. I guess it's still an awesome realization to me that when we take the pain that comes very close to killing us and begin to use it to reach out to others in the name and love of Christ, we come into full service and ministry for God and for mankind. What a ministry we have!

The year I was going through my divorce, one of my friends, who sounded like one of Job's friends, wrote: "I watched from a distance as you changed your emphasis from the family to a specialized ministry on behalf of others in pain." A few lines down he noted, "I fear you made an enormous mistake."

Perhaps my old friend, I did indeed make an enormous mistake, but God didn't. He knew that the day would come when I would share with countless others the physical pain of my jaw (the TMJ disorder) and the emotional pain of my brokenness and grief losses. I would share them in order to serve and to minister in an even greater capacity to hurting families. Instead of changing my emphasis, I have, in fact, intensified it.

If you are wounded, you are still a part of some family no matter how sick and broken or how healthy and whole those relationships are. Each time I get a letter from a wounded soul or talk with one who's suffered greatly, I realize there are a thousand ways for a heart to be wounded and broken. But equally true is the fact that there are many ways for God to bring us into wellness and recovery. The thrilling reward of being wounded is that it lets us be a part of God's healing toward others.

Before I leave this chapter about our God-calling and our choice to become wounded healers, I feel I must say a few words of encouragement to you who are young and have not yet suffered and to those of you who are in your

middle or later years and have come through this journey virtually unscathed and unscarred by the wounding
process.

In this chapter I may have inadvertantly led you to
believe that unless you have been severely wounded you
cannot be used of God. But that is simply not so.

I remember a conversation I had some years ago with
a very successful man in full-time Christian service. He
was enumerating the various kinds of grief anguish I'd
gone through with the deaths of my baby, grandfather,
and mother, and of the physical pain I was suffering with
my jaw and TMJ. He was struggling with all of this for he
had concluded from what he knew of my pain process
and from what he had read of the sufferings of so many
great Old and New Testament people, pastors, and missionaries. He felt that because he had not suffered the
grief loss of anyone close to him or known any serious
illness firsthand, perhaps God was not going to use him
in a truly significant way.

Two things immediately sprang into my mind. He was
already blessed and being used of God in a profound
and powerful way, even without the suffering.

And second, I told him that I believed even though
he'd not as yet suffered the agony of the wounding process, if pain and suffering were to enter his life big time,
God would lead him through that dark river of pain,
accompany him to the other side and give him some
unique credentials for a greater and more intensified
ministry.

Without God's calling to be a wounded healer, the
wounding would make no sense at all. We would never
find any sense or meaning in pain. Often it's been said

that when one loses not only hope but purpose or meaning in life, *all* is lost. In contrast to that bleak alternative, I am now relishing the mission God has so generously given to so many of us. In the beautiful words of Nouwen:

Shared pain is no longer paralyzing but mobilizing, when understood as a way to liberation: "When we become aware that we do not have to escape our pains, but that we can mobilize them into a common search for life, those very pains are transformed from expressions of despair into signs of hope."[5]

And near the end of his book he leaves us with:

"We do not know where we will be two, ten or twenty years from now. What we can know, however, is that man suffers and that a sharing of suffering can make us move forward."[6]

Ah yes, dear Henri Nouwen, "those very pains are transformed from expression of despair into signs of hope."

I choose to be a wounded healer.

SIX

I CHOOSE TO PRAY LARGE PRAYERS

Pray the largest prayers
Pray not for crutches but for wings!
Rt. Rev. Phillips Brooks D.D.,
1835–1893

From the second these words startled my heart and shouted up at me from the pages of Phillips Brooks's devotional *Perennials* (New York: E. P. Dutton, Copyrighted 1898, Published 1909), I realized that I've spent most of my adult life praying small, infinitesimally small prayers. The memory of those scrawny, rather anemic prayers elbowed their way into my mind and forced me to acknowledge that the spiritual pride I once felt concerning my glorious "ability" to pray and the insightful "contents" of those prayers, was gone. I had no self-grandiose illusions left. My prayer life was definitely of the narrow-gauged variety.

How awful. I've prayed for crutches instead of wings almost every time I've prayed. Oh, the influential power of words, especially the power of Phillips Brooks's words. They have never failed to sway my heart and pull it upward.

How awful. I've prayed for crutches instead of wings almost every time I've prayed.

Over the years now, many fine gifted writers have made me very rich. They've contributed to my wealth intellectually, emotionally and, most definitely, spiritually. There are those writers, however, who stand way out in front of other illustrious and glorious authors because they seem to have the ability to probe and penetrate deeply, straight to my heart, matching my need, whatever it might be, with their healing words. Those kinds of writers seem to have a way of heavily impacting me.

I'm not merely charmed or captivated by their writing. Rather *their* words bring me to the center stage of *my* life. They force me to deal with my need to make changes, my need to choose different options and my need to revise my attitude. More often than not, these writers set Psalm 51:10—"Create in me a clean heart, O God; and renew a right spirit within me" (KJV)—clearly in my sights, and my determination to have a clean heart and a right spirit (attitude) is strengthened.

One such writer, who never fails to stir my mentally lazy bones and my indifferent eyes and ears to meeting the ongoing challenge, is Dr. Phillips Brooks, the author of the words, "Pray the largest prayers."

I am filled with a rapturous wonder when I see how God works through his people. Here is a man who lived and died in the 1800s, long before most of us were born. A man who preached and wrote to congregations both in Philadelphia and Boston, he lived during the time of the Civil War, spoke out against slavery and was a twenty-eight-year-old pastor of a large church when President Abraham Lincoln was assassinated.

The life and ambiance of Dr. Brooks is beautifully described in Harold Ivan Smith's book *Movers and Shakers* (Old Tappan, New Jersey: Revell, 1988) so I'm now only one of many in my generation, who is deeply touched, tenderly convicted and marvelously comforted by this man's wisdom and godly life. Dr. Brooks's sermons, his scribbled-down notes and his classic lyrics to "O Little Town of Bethlehem" continue, after all these years, to stir hearts. When he died in 1893, he was eulogized by his brother, the Reverend Arthur Brooks, D.D., in these words:

From God he came;
With God he walked;
God's world he loved;
God's church he led
God's blessed Son he followed;
God's nearness he enjoyed;
Now with God he dwells.[1]

As I write, Phillips Brooks's tattered and time-worn devotional lays open before me. It was rescued by a friend who was searching out old books for me from a minister's garage sale. I love it for it speaks to me as much as if it was a huge, leather-bound volume or a whole set of current encyclopedias.

The decision to stop my small-scale praying and pray large prayers came after my heart heard what Dr. Brooks was saying when he wrote:

Pray the largest prayers

Pray not for crutches but for wings.[2]

He continued on by commenting, "Oh! Do not pray just that God will keep you from breaking down, and somehow, anyhow, help you to stagger and stumble through."

How often my whole mind-set during prayer has been exactly that. "Lord, just get me through, one day at a time. Somehow, anyhow, drag me by the hair if you have to, just get me through."

Brooks's finely honed words burned deeply yet kindly into my soul, moving and convicting me and at the same time giving hope, encouragement and instilling the determination in me to press upward on the steep slopes of the invisible mountain called prayer.

Yesterday, I was fascinated as I went through Phillips Brooks's entire book and found other sharply focused things he had written in regard to praying large prayers. Here are some excerpts (the titles are mine). I have deliberately tried to refrain from expanding and expounding on them too much because I know you are perfectly capable of hearing your own messages from the printed words. I'm even more aware of the fact that the Holy Spirit knows where we are, what we need and when to bring the most salient points to our attention.

ON WHAT A LARGE PRAYER REALLY IS:

Pray for his light and life to come and fill you, that you may live like him, that you may tread temptation under foot and walk across it into holiness; that you may be enthusiastically good, that you may shine forth with his light on other lives.[3]

For a couple of years now my awakening prayer has been, Fill me with your light and life, Lord. Why? For the reasons listed above.

ON UNANSWERED PRAYER:

If our answered prayers are precious to us, I sometimes think our *un*answered prayers are more precious still.

Those give us God's blessings; these, if we will, may lead us to God.[4]

ON PRAYING FOR GOD'S BEST:

Could not Christ have answered your prayer?
No, he could not.
The thing you asked for was not the absolutely best, and therefore, he could not give it.
Back of how many unanswered prayers lies that divine impossibility.[5]

ON THE LARGE AND LOFTIEST OF PRAYERS:

Let us try, if we are really Christians who believe that our Lord has ascended into heaven, to enter into his heavenly life by the largeness and loftiness of the prayers that we bring to him.

Not comfort, not spiritual rest, not freedom from pain here or hereafter,

Not these, but the chance, the power, the will to glorify God our Father in our lives, as he, the perfect Son, did in his. This we may ask.[6]

ON PRAYING A VERY LARGE PRAYER:

"Lord, that we might receive our sight." How deep these words are! Our sight!—a sight which, though we never saw with it, is really ours—the sight with which we were made to see.

Not once in all the gospels is it written that Christ passed by a prayer like that and did not answer it.[7]

ON WHAT NOT TO PRAY FOR:

Do not pray for easy lives; pray to be stronger men. Do not pray for tasks equal to your powers; pray for powers equal to your tasks.

If the life you have chosen to be your life is really worthy of you, it involves self-sacrifice and pain.

If your Jerusalem is your sacred city, there is certainly a cross in it.

Ask God to fill you with himself, and then calmly look up and go on.

Disappointment, mortification, misconception, enmity, pain, death, these may come to you but if they come to you in doing your duty, it is all right.[8]

ON PRAYING LARGE PRAYERS EVEN WHEN WE DON'T FEEL LIKE PRAYING:

Just as the bird is a bird still although it cannot sing, and the rose is still a rose although it's red grows dull and faded in some dark, close room where it is compelled to grow,

So the Christian is a Christian still even though his soul is dark with doubt, and he goes staggering on, fearing every moment that he will fall, never daring to look up and hope.[9]

ON PRAYING LARGE PRAYERS:

We do not pray God to love us; but we do pray that we may see his love that we shall love him back again, and be saved by loving.[10]

ON PRAYING WHEN WE CAN'T SEE WHERE WE ARE GOING:

How large a part of our Godward life is troubled, not by clear landmarks seen afar off in the promised land,

But as travellers climb a mountain peak, by putting footstep after footstep slowly and patiently into the foot prints which someone going before us has planted deep into the pathless snow.[11]

ON WHY IT'S SO IMPORTANT TO PRAY LARGE PRAYERS NOW:

The ship is out on mid-ocean, and it is midnight, and the storm is wild. The winds are savage, and the sea is terrible.

We say the ship is struggling for her life. But, tell me, where was the real struggle of the vessel?

Was it not long ago on the hillside where her timbers grew, and in the shipyard where her nails were driven?

Then it was decided whether she was to go to the bottom or come safely to her port.

So, as I look forward, I can see you, on some day in the years to come, wrestling the great temptation, or trembling like a reed under the great sorrow of your life, a temptation or a sorrow of which you have as yet no conception. The crisis may be years away.

But the real struggle is not then, but now, here, on this quiet day and in these quiet weeks.

Now it is being decided whether, in the day of your supreme sorrow or temptation you shall miserably fail or gloriously conquer.[12]

As I've absorbed these pungent yet eloquent words about praying and have been consciously choosing to pray those large prayers, the literary work of another "dear friend" I never met, Martha Snell Nicholson, an invalid for twenty-five years and a woman after God's own heart, came to mind. She wrote many poems and some prose. One poem was about God answering a large prayer of hers but the prayer was not answered in the way Martha thought.

THE THORN

I stood, a mendicant of God,
Before his royal throne,
And begged him for one priceless gift
For me to call my own.

I took the gift from out his hand,
But as I would depart
I cried, "But Lord, this is a thorn,
And it has pierced my heart!

"This is a strange and hurtful gift
Which Thou hast given me."
He said, "I love to give good gifts,
I gave My best to thee."

I took it home, and though at first
The cruel thorn hurt sore,
As long years passed I grew at last
To love it more and more.

I learned he never gives a thorn
Without this added grace:
He takes the thorn to pin aside
The veil which hides his face![13]

---

*I can count on the fact that God
meets me wherever I am.*

I may be laid aside in a sick room as Martha was for so
many years with one dreaded disease after another or
smack in the middle of rush hour traffic, but I can count
on the fact that God meets me wherever I am. God holds
communion, that blessed sacrament, with me. He comes
to me whether I'm homeless and living in a cardboard
box under a viaduct or fortunate enough to be in a warm
home surrounded by loved ones and things of beauty.
God holds communion with me whether I am standing

on the brink of war, the edge of bankruptcy, the threat of cancer or the verge of madness. He tenderly holds my whole being with the same love whether I'm reading by my fireside, laughing with my dearest loved one, enjoying financial security or being delighted by the comfort of emotional stability. (It does seem easier to trust him when things go very well!) No matter how I feel or what my circumstances are, God meets me where I am.

My heart was fearful as our country went to war in the Middle East against the Iraqi leader, Saddam Hussein. Only God knew how long and at what price before peace was ultimately restored in the region. During those same months, my fears also included a number of serious personal and business concerns. They loomed up like large wild beasts charging straight for me. I was hard pressed to see the "One between me and them."

Although I'm against war just as I am against death, disease and divorce (and these things scare me to death), I believe that God meets us even at these times. And I suspect he finds us best when we are wandering and grasping about in the dark basement of our house of reality. He meets our needs precisely where they are the greatest and where our fears lie the heaviest in our hearts. As the psalmist reminded us, God *knows* when we sit or stand and, even more astoundingly, what we are going to say *before* we say it (Psalm 139). He knows us inside and out.

It is on these fearful and disturbing days that I find myself praying, almost shouting the largest of prayers. Ironically, my largest prayers for several years now have been two frantically uttered words: *Jesus, intervene.*

Once in a while, even when praying, *Jesus, intervene,* I
lapse into my old small-time prayer habits. I find myself
going through a silly exercise in prayer which includes
an agenda for God to follow. It's embarrassing to recall
all the prayers that I've prayed in this presumptuous
manner. These prayers sound something like this:

Dear Lord,

Ah, with all due respect, I wish to make my
needs known to you. Now here is the thing that
scares me the most (I give him a blazingly detailed
description).

And here, dear Lord, is my exciting "druthers
plan" starting with the **A** solution. If you can't do
the **A** plan then, here is my rather common boring
plan **B.** Now if that proves unacceptable, here
then is my "If-you-must, you-must" plan **C.** (Personally, I hope you go with plan **A.**)

And Lord, however you want to answer me is
fine, but of the **A, B** or **C** solutions, I'd really appreciate your concentrating on the **A** plan. It's
preferred. Of course if you choose to go with **B** or
C I'm sure I'll adjust.

Thank you, Lord.

It's utterly amazing how God usually does his own
thing and completely disregards my "astute" *A, B* or *C*
recommendations. He answers me far better—you
guessed it—with *Q, R* and *S.*

I wrote in *The Inheritance* (Austin, TX: Balcony, 1989)
of my mother when she was a student in Central Bible
College. Dedicated to becoming a missionary to Africa,
she fell in love with a student at the same school who was
dedicated to becoming a missionary to China. Mother's

diary was filled with her *A, B* and *C* solutions to God about their unique dilemma. They loved each other but their relationship was not without conflict, as mother put it to God in her diary, "If we love each other, surely Lord, you do not want us to part. If he is for me, you will not let him think he belongs in China! Make him see the need of Africa, bring it before him Lord."

This was her first-choice *A* plan, and clearly it was her druther plan that she was hoping the Lord would choose. But not taking any chances, she outlined plan *B* a couple of pages later in her diary. The *B* plan was about her alternative of going home to heaven. She wrote:

> I **long** to be with Jesus. Perhaps I'm too selfish and am trying to shrink from my duty, to get away from all these testing times and trials that must come to every Christian. I feel as though I'm a coward, and of course I am, but oh, how I want to go home to heaven.

Next, Mother was running true to human form because with a heavy spirit and broken heart she penned plan *C.* And she meant every line of it.

> If I'm to go to Africa **alone,** with no one to help me, no human love to sustain me, with no arm of flesh to lean upon, God knows all about it.
>
> If it must be that I go to Africa without a companion, God will have to give me more strength, more of his grace, more of his love and more of himself. If I will have no human flesh to help me, God knows I will have to look to him more often and trust him fully.

If this is your dear will, Lord, make me willing
to give up all.

God did not deem it fit to address himself to Mother's
A, B or *C* solutions for the rest of her three years at Bible
college. Naturally, three weeks *after* graduation God answered her prayers, and naturally he did not answer *A, B*
or *C,* but with *Q, R* and *S* of his own making and choice.
God simply gave these dedicated, would-be-missionaries,
his best for their lives.

In the weeks after their graduation, both *failed* their
physical tests, which were absolutely necessary to pass before either could go to Africa or China. The following
September they were married, accepted a call to pastor a
church in Saginaw, Michigan, and a year and a half later
I, the first of their three children, was born in true *Q, R,
S* fashion.

Upon reflection, I find my impulsive need to "help"
God out by giving him my solutions and well-worked-out
timetables a bit amusing. Once in a while I'm amazed
that God goes ahead and gives me my plan *A* answer. Of
course, I doubt he really needs even my best or sincerest
A, B or *C* plans still he answers. Perhaps I give God my
plans because I am so fearful (like I am today) that my
prayers will go to heaven and just pile up in great stacks
and be stored somewhere waiting for his attention, even
though, intellectually, I know this is not true. Perhaps I
come up with these solutions not so much to have God
hear them as to give myself some feeling that I'm *doing*
something instead of just sitting back twiddling my
thumbs.

I love what Amy Carmichael, the lifelong missionary to

India, wrote about accepting the answers to our prayers (with or without our *A, B* or *C* plans).

> I once wrote that God always answers us in the deeps, not in the shallows of our prayers. Hasn't it been so with you?
>
> One of the hardest things in our secret prayer life is to accept with joy and not with grief, the answers to our deepest prayers. At least I have found it so.
>
> It was a long time before I discovered that *whatever came was the answer.* I had expected something so different that I did not recognize it when it came.
>
> And he doesn't explain. He trusts us not to be offended; that's all.[14]

Our heavenly Father hears *all* our prayers (even the *A, B* and *C* kinds) and at times gives us our plan *A* answer. We can rest assured that God *answers* us all out of his dear love for each of us, his children. We may be unable to fathom the exact nature of his plans but we can choose to trust him. And believe me, God can be trusted.

It's also true, and the scriptures document my beliefs here, that there are many ways to pray large prayers, but one very definite stipulation in praying is that we must *pray according to God's will.* The problem with this is we may not have a single clue as to what his will is. This is the time to give God and the Holy Spirit the benefit of the doubt and the simplicity of our desires by praying, *Jesus, intervene.*

I have noticed when I pray for wings instead of crutches the largest of my prayers are not determined by my loquaciousness or the prayer's length but, rather, by the attitude and the intensity of the heart.

Ironically, the most significant prayers of mine—those which were gigantic in size, those which reached the farthest points and those which brought in the greatest wide-opened and sizable results—were made up of a few urgently whispered words:

> intervene,
> deliver,
> rescue,
> save,
> heal,
> restore,
> carry,
> hold.

And on some occasions, when my emotions felt colossally damaged, when my strength and inner resources had ebbed out of me, it was enough—more than enough—to breathe one name, the name of *Jesus*. Why? Because according to Paul's writing to the Romans, what happens at this juncture in our prayer life is simple but quite wonderful.

The Holy Spirit sees our paralysis and our inability to put into words the overwhelming pain and grief-needs we are feeling and he takes over. The Holy Spirit does the pleading to God in our behalf. He *prays* for us:

> We do not know how to pray worthily as sons of God, but his Spirit within us is actually praying for us in those agonizing longings which never find words. And God who knows the heart's secrets understands, of course, the Spirit's intention as he prays for those who love God (Rom. 8:26–27 J. B. Phillips).

Which brings us right back to praying not only large prayers but prayers in Jesus' name and God's.

This past November our hearts and home were blessed and graced by sharing Thanksgiving dinner with a vibrant young couple, Kim and Tom. The ambiance of the whole evening—from the flowers, candlelight and roast turkey to our guests' conversation and laughter as we sat at a round table in our living room—was warm with the spirit of balcony love.

After dinner, Francis and Tom departed in the direction of our family room and Kim and I cleaned away the dinner plates. Then we both felt drawn back to the table.

We slipped comfortably into a conversation which covered all sorts of subjects. Though there must be twenty years difference in our ages (*she's* the younger one), it was a beautiful time. We met in her parent's wonderful church only a short time ago, so there's no long history of friendship between us. Yet, our hearts opened to each other in that much needed and healing way as it sometimes happens when women find themselves together. We sat leisurely at the table talking of the invigorating events of our lives and of the inspiring people God had gently placed in our paths for our healing and restoration.

An hour or so later, the candles burning down to the crystal holders, we eased into sharing the full range of our most private and grave hurts. We talked of what was presently plunging us into the fiery sea of pain and what ugly thing was stalking us in the shadows and what was looming ahead of us. In the intimacy of this time we wondered how God would guide, how he would direct, how he would bring us through the dreary weariness of it all, and what joys or sorrows the approaching year would hold for both of us.

As we were leaving the table to join our husbands in

the other room, I mentioned to Kim that I'd be praying for her daily in the next few months. Well aware of the rugged path ahead of her and of the difficult (and possibly destructive) encounters that were about to rain on her life's parade, I asked her what she wanted me to pray specifically about for her.

She was thoughtful for a moment and then replied, "Pray for direction. Pray that I'll know God's will in all of this . . . yes, pray for direction."

And so I have. But as soon as Kim said the word *direction*, I thought, "Yes, me too, Lord. Isn't godly direction, or at least *some* kind of map or forecast for the future, what we all want and pray for?"

The gifted actor, Kevin Costner, commented on the confusing time in his life between college graduation, marriage, acting classes and his menial jobs: "I prayed, Jesus, give me direction!" How real.

We pray for God to give us direction and to let us know his will. As believers we are confident that he has chartered our course and secured our ultimate destination. But so often along the way, we're in that "not-quite-sure" time in our lives when we wonder (sometimes in panic) whether we are following the course our heavenly Father has mapped out. What if we can't find our compass and we've lost the charts? What if there's nothing in the instruction booklet for this particular situation? Lord, what is your will?

All of us know the best way, the really essential way to pray large prayers is to pray steadfastly in God's will. That's so easy to say and so hard to do. In fact, let's say God's will came out from behind some tree, stuck his foot out and I tripped over it. I wonder if I'd be astute or wise enough to know, as I was falling, that it was his will?

Mmmmmmmhm. It's still the sixty-four-dollar question: what do you want me to do? Dr. Sam Shoemaker wrote:

> Underlying and running through all our prayers of whatever kind, must be this big one, "What shall I do, Lord?"
>
> Don't pray to escape trouble. Don't pray to be comfortable in your emotions. Pray to do the will of God in every situation. Nothing else is worth praying for.[15]

A couple of weeks ago I was pondering the enigma and trying to find some garden-fresh insights on knowing God's will and discerning the direction the Lord wanted me to go while praying. My husband, Francis, said suddenly, "Darling, listen to this!" He proceeded to read aloud two very familiar prayers of Jesus. One prayer was in John, the other in Mark.

Francis had grasped a significant message about praying in and for God's will. He had seen something in those two prayers that I don't recall any pastor (including my own preacher father) pointing out when giving a sermon about God's will.

As Francis walked me through what he had seen in both Jesus' prayers, I was thrilled with the revelation of such a plain yet beautiful truth. But at the same time I felt a little foolish that these truths had zipped neatly over the top of my head for all these years. I couldn't even give my favorite retort, "I knew that."

Over the next few days I found myself reading and rereading both of those prayers and tracking them down in every translation and paraphrase I own.

Jesus' prayer as preserved in John, the seventeenth chapter, is of vital significance. The prayer was said in the Upper Room following the Last Supper, on the same night Jesus was arrested. The horror of the crucifixion had begun.

The disciples had to be terribly uncertain not only about what their future held but whether they even *had* a future. It must have been impossible for them to conceptualize the events that were about to take place.

But Jesus, understanding all of this so well, gathered his men together at the Passover Supper, and during the meal, he prepared his disciples for his approaching death with deeply confounding lessons. They could scarcely take it all in. He talked of going away; yet, he told them he'd always be with them. He assured them that they would receive help and comfort from the Holy Spirit and that the world would hate them so much that it was of paramount importance that they love each other. One can only try to imagine the wild melee of thoughts and questions which must have raced through each man's mind.

After their supper and apparently just before they all left to walk across the Cedron Valley to the Garden of Gethsemane, Jesus concluded his words to his much-beloved disciples by praying for himself, for his present followers, and for all of us who would become his disciples down through the ages.

You can read for yourself the whole prayer in the seventeenth chapter of John, but here are Jesus' major petitions to his Father. In his prayer he specifically asks:

to glorify him, the son, and

to honor him,

to keep all of *us* in God's care,

to not take us out of this world but to keep us safe from Satan's power, to make us pure and holy by teaching us God's words of truth,

to help all of us, the disciples and all future believers, to be of one heart and one mind.

It was here, Francis pointed out, that Jesus' prayer was remarkably similar or tantamount to our *A, B,* or *C* approach in praying. (Only offhand, as I reread Jesus' prayer, I see it's more like his prayer had an *A* through *Z* plan in it.) Jesus clearly stated his wants, his wishes and his desires to God, the Father. But the most striking thing about this prayer is that the heavenly Father, as history has since showed, granted each request the way Jesus presented it to him. God gave Jesus what he asked for. It is a moving example of our praying with *A, B, C* in mind and getting *A, B,* and *C.*

Francis also suggested that perhaps sometimes when we pray, we can be so in tune to the Lord and so connected to the beautiful Holy Spirit that we are *already* praying in the will of God. And so God does, indeed, answer us exactly as we petitioned, giving us what we wanted.

Lately, I have watched as I've been frantically praying, *Jesus, intervene,* or giving the Lord my *A, B,* and *C* plans. Because my call for help or my plan was in line, or in harmony as others have said, with God's will and timing, I've seen God answer in a matter of minutes, other times in a day or within a week. Nevertheless, his answers were pretty incredible evidence to the wonder of praying large prayers and getting *wings* instead of crutches. Seeing a house sold within four days of listing it in a very depressed market; seeing a shattered relationship healed and restored; seeing a large order for product come into Balcony Publishing from a totally unexpected source;

seeing a loved one deal with abuse or break the chains of an addiction; seeing God provide emotional relief, even comfort, to the overwhelming despair of my depression: these things have increased my faith, my ability to trust God, and have put credibility into my prayer life. Praying large prayers, like *Jesus, intervene,* or for "wings instead of crutches" has brought new meaning to the Isaiah passage: "But they that wait upon the LORD shall renew their strength; they shall mount up with wings" (Is. 40:31 KJV).

Let's go back to the Upper Room on that momentous night in the lives of Jesus and his disciples.

You will recall that after Jesus ended prayer in the Upper Room, all of the disciples sang a hymn and left to walk to the Mount of Olives.

They reached an olive grove called the Garden of Gethsemane, and Jesus instructed most of his disciples to stay in one place, while he took Peter, James and John with him as he had done on other occasions.

It is impossible for me to imagine the avalanche of guilt and pain which bore down upon Jesus' body. It must have crushed his mind and soul, and it must have been utterly foreign and unfathomable to him. Even though Peter, James and John were his closest companions, Jesus' weight of sorrow and grief was such that he knew he had to be alone to pray: "My soul is very sorrowful, even to death; remain here, and watch" (Mark 14:34 RSV).

He probably left Peter, James and John in the shelter of some large rocks or well-placed olive trees as he pressed further on to a more secluded place in the garden. He was feeling and carrying the tremendous burden of the whole world's sin and the evil and pain of all the ages. Under that kind of weight, when he could *walk* no more, he fell to the ground and began his second prayer of that night. It was the most anguished prayer of his life.

It is not terribly surprising that this Gethsemane prayer of Jesus was quite brief. The agony of the world had rained its onslaught of hail down on him, pelting his heart, depleting his strength. I'd say that Jesus' depression must have been full of unbelievable pressure, hot and scalding, leaving him feeling peeled and skinless. There wasn't time for him in this tortured prayer to be eloquent. Nor was there time to begin as usual with words of praise and thanksgiving to his Father. Jesus was being well shaken by the death throes of his life.

He did not pray in the established or traditionally accepted ways of the high priests. He was a completely vulnerable man, a heart-hemorrhaging man. His sweat glistened red on his face and then gathered together like great drops of blood and fell, staining the earth beneath him. His prayer had to be brief because there was just too much pain ferociously beating against his whole being.

Here, in Gethsemane, writhing in the grip of the fiercest battle he'd ever known, Jesus prays his second prayer—the largest of life and his three-year ministry. The scriptures detail those moments: "And he went forward a little, and fell on the ground, and prayed that, if it were possible, the hour might pass from him. And he said, 'Abba, Father, all things are possible unto thee; take away this cup from me: nevertheless not what I will, but what thou wilt' " (Mark 14:35–36 KJV).

Your will, not mine, God. Your will, not mine.

See the moment. Here was Jesus, a beloved son, boldly and freely rushing to his Father, pleading for this miserable cup of pain to pass from his lips. And then, almost in the same breath, he utters the wonderful and liberating word, *nevertheless.* "Nevertheless," he cried out, "Abba, Father, it is not what I want but what you want. Not my will but yours."

Lying at the very core of Jesus' heart was that large prayer: "Your will not mine." Bolting down through the centuries like fierce lightning it illuminates our prayer life for us to see and to pass on to future generations. *Your will, not mine, God. Your will, not mine.*

The truth Francis wanted me to see was that in his first "Upper Room" prayer, Jesus was confident enough of the loving relationship between him and his Father to make his wants clearly known. He asked for *A, B,* and *C* and God granted each and every one of his petitions. But Jesus' "Gethsemane" prayer, his second prayer that night, shows us that he was more than willing to risk praying the largest of prayers and to leave the outcome of his holocaust in God the Father's hands. *Thy will be done. . . . not mine, but thine.* Jesus left no doubt that he wanted out. He wanted to be released from the racking agony of this most dreadful hour. But towering above his wants was the truest desire of his heart.

The final words of his largest prayer came at the turning point for Jesus. From then until the crucifixion, his attitude was one of acceptance and resolve, even in the face of extreme humiliation and the most hideous of all physical torture.

In my mind's eye I see him. He has absorbed the words "Not my will but yours, Father" into his whole being. I see him firmly setting his jaw and, with great effort, slowly rising from the tear-soaked ground, brushing off his robe, standing tall, smoothing his wet, matted hair away from his face. He straightens his shoulders with majestic resolve and takes slow but sure steps down the hill toward his sleeping disciples. He is surrounded by a sense of divine tranquility. An aura of peace is as distinctive and recognizable about him now as it must have been when he was twelve years old answering his worried mother's questions in the temple, calmly assuring her that he was in his Father's house, doing his Father's will, as his Father had called him to do.

In this single night, Jesus prayed two prayers: the Upper Room prayer with his disciples, specific and detailed, where God granted all that he asked; and the Gethsemane prayer, where he prayed alone and left all roads open to the Father.

So I see a triumphant Jesus as he finds his way around the olive trees and climbs down the hill to gather his disciples together and to face the mob and the awaiting holocaust. He has an unwavering trust in his Father and an unflinching sense of mission twined together like a mantle around his shoulders. He is at peace, even in the midst of the raging battle of Calvary, for the son *knows* and *trusts* his Father. One can tell by his kingly carriage, by the glory which shimmers lightly from his eyes and by the sureness of his steps, that all is well within the man. All is well within.

The sight of him makes my heart want to burst into singing the old hymn by Horatio G. Spafford:

> When peace, like a river, attendeth my way,
> When sorrows like sea billows roll;
> Whatever my lot, Thou has taught me to say,
> It is well, it is well with my soul.

How amazing for all of God's children. God's plans are still the very best for us, even as we pray our *A, B, C* prayers, petitioning God for the needs of our life, as we see it, or as we, alone in our Gethsemane, pray for this cup to pass and pray the largest of prayers, "not my will, but thine be done."

We can get up from our knees or from the blood and tear-drenched ground beneath, confident that we can trust the loving plans our Father has for us. We can leave our Upper Room or our Garden of Gethsemane to meet the enemy with renewed strength, with courage and with the same peace Jesus had, a peace which certainly is beyond all understanding. And then, like the Lord, we can walk into battle knowing all is well within us.

As long as God gives us breath here on earth, whenever we choose to pray large prayers, that choice brings about the most significant and dramatic changes in our attitudes that we will ever experience on this earthly journey.

Perhaps in heaven we may be allowed to view our life here, and if that's true, I believe we will mentally see and remember with great joy the significant times we prayed large prayers and God gave us wings instead of crutches. He gave us those wings because he knew what we *really* wanted was for *his* will to be done.

We shall also recall with great pleasure, even if others did not see it, how God answered our largest prayers, how he filled us with his life and light, so that much of our time here . . .

We *did* live like him,
We *did* tread temptation underfoot and walk across it into holiness,
We *were* enthusiastically good and
God's light *did* shine through us with his brightness on the lives of others around us!
So, I pray today, dear Lord,
Don't let me get away with praying small, weak, spineless prayers. Keep me afraid of smallness.
Don't let me become so paralyzed and intimidated by the terror of my Gethsemane cup or the loneliness of my lost and broken dreams that I forget to trust your intervention and direction.
Don't let me lose my focus on the high priority of gladly surrendering to *your* will. "Mesh our will totally into yours," as my sister Marilyn prayed today,
And don't let my soul ever forget how good you are to me. Keep me resting in the peace of this truth.
And, oh yes, please, dear Lord,
daily remind me to pray *largely!*

SEVEN

I CHOOSE TO TAKE ACTION

The usually well-organized woman in charge of the large three-day retreat came up to our hotel room and was obviously in the process of unraveling at the seams. Her main speaker for the afternoon time slot had been delayed by bad weather, and so she was standing before me, wringing her hands and asking if I would fill in for her. I'd already spoken the night before and earlier that morning and was to speak again, ending the conference the following night. But the woman was in a tough spot, so I did my best to calm her and assured her that I'd be happy to do it. Gratefully, she relayed the details: in about an hour from now the first speaker would go on, there would be a short break, and then I'd follow for the main meeting.

I hastily pulled together some thoughts, and Francis and I walked over to the convention center. We found a side door and slipped into the big auditorium. The session was well underway with some excellent musicians doing a great job leading singing. Then, a middle-aged gentleman, the first speaker, was introduced. I immediately felt a little anxious for him. The audience was made up of close to two thousand women, and because I've spoken to all–male audiences occasionally, I know a little about the threat and the pressure involved in speaking to an audience dominated by the opposite sex. But as he began his speech, I became more than a little anxious; I was alarmed.

The man was giving his version of a motivational speech he had obviously taken from a well-known personality and lecturer but without any apparent regard for the fact that his audience was completely made up of women. He proceeded to tell one "joke" after another, all bad-mouthing women. He even included some crude remarks about his wife.

It was easy to catch the rising hostility of the women in the audience. I could feel some women mentally moving toward lynching the man on the spot while others were mentally walking en masse toward the exits.

I kept thinking that surely the speaker would turn the thing around or perhaps see that the reason his audience was not responding with laughter at his humorous verbal attacks on women was because it just wasn't *that* funny to them or the words sounded too much like what they heard at home.

But the man never caught on. Here he was on stage going full-steam ahead with his prepared speech, never noticing that he was the only one who thought his material humorous or helpful.

During my thirty years of public speaking, I've studied audiences from behind the podium or pulpit. And like other speakers, pastors, and musicians I know, I watch every movement and each nuance, no matter how slight, of the people before me. No yawn escapes me, no glance at one's watch (no matter how slyly done) is missed. I even evaluate the applause and the stillness of an audience long after I've stepped off the stage. So whether I'm speaking or not, this old habit of mine to observe is a part of every meeting of any kind.

The women around Francis and I were moving and shifting uncomfortably in their seats, and a low murmuring was rumbling through the whole auditorium. I glanced over at my husband with a look that asked him if this was really as bad as I thought it was or was I just throwing a temperamental fit over nothing? His look reassured me that I was not losing my mind or the ability to read an audience accurately.

The speaker went on, quite oblivious to the fact that he'd lost his audience. I'd been consumed with assessing the man's material and the audience reaction when suddenly reality hit me—I was up next.

I'd put together for my part of the evening a rather informal nonstructured talk for women—something I love doing. But in the hour the man had been speaking two thousand women had gone from I'm-so-thrilled-to-be-here to Why-am-I-here? It was scary to know that I'd be up at the podium next. It was not a hard act to follow, as they say; it was absolutely impossible to follow. I turned to Francis, and bordering on hysterics, I declared, "I can't go up on that stage and follow this. The women are so mad at him I don't think I can pull them back into listening or hearing anything!"

Francis was sympathetic to my plight. He's been at enough of my speaking engagements and has heard enough speakers in his own time that he knew much of what I was feeling and experiencing about being the next speaker, but he didn't say anything.

Finally, with my state of panic approaching seizure level, I leaned over again to him and urgently asked, "How am I gonna follow this? What in the world am I going to say?"

I'll never forget Francis' body language or his amusing words. He lovingly reached over, gently patted my white-knuckled clenched fist, gave me his warmest thousand-watt smile, which positively shone with confidence, and whispered, "Just get up there and . . . do something."

"Oh, that's great!" I laughed right out loud. "Do something?" That kind of brilliance is hard to come by. "Easy for you to say." I stopped laughing and went back to biting my cuticles.

But the funny thing was that after the speaker drew his talk mercifully to a close, and after the break and after the group of musicians performed, I did exactly what Francis had told me to do. I got up there on that stage and did something. Mind you, I'm not sure what exactly . . . only that I didn't run away or disappear out the nearest exit like I truly longed to do. I stayed.

I can't believe it yet. I faced the moment and forced my legs to carry me up to the front, up the stairs, and onto the stage. I still don't have a clue as to what I said or what, if any, lasting impact I presented or whether my audience thought it was a meaningful experience or not. I just know that I chose to take action. Sink or swim, I had to *do* something. I had to take action.

When we choose to go for new attitudes, that's great. But we can't stay there. We should not stop with that first step. Merely choosing a new and different attitude is not enough. We must take action if we are ever going to expect change in our lives and experience any measure of healing.

"Just get up there and . . . do something."

In the last two years I've given this "Blue Blanket" talk to many people, many times all over the country. The response from people in Florida, Minnesota, Oregon, Texas, Colorado, Virginia, Kansas, California, and back to Florida again has been very confirming for me. Apparently, many of you are ready to make some personal decisions to choose new attitudes in regard to glittering images, hurts, blue blankets, wounded healers, and praying large prayers. I hope you are also willing not to stop there but to go on with a plan of action.

I wish this book could end with our agreeing that all we have to do is think realistically about our lives, then simply choose new attitudes, and decide to look at new patterns. But we must always follow choice with action if our choice is to be of any ultimate significance.

If we are created not merely to survive but to live abundant lives and experience recovery, then we must go beyond a mental decision. We must take assertive action.

I can hear some of you saying, "Oh, but Joyce, after what I've been through, I'm emotionally exhausted. I'm bone tired. I don't have the strength to 'take action.'"

I confess I know about that kind of tiredness. I constantly suffer battle fatigue. Like you, I'm deeply scarred, and though the wounds are well on their way to healing, the scars remain painful to touch and I always fear that those scars might be torn open again. This sense of disconnectedness, as Nouwen calls it, has left most of us incredibly weary. Ask me what I'd like to do now about "taking action," and my first response is absolutely zip. Zilch. Zero. Nothing.

When we choose to go for new attitudes, that's great. But we can't stay there.

Actually, I'd like to sit down in a comfortable overstuffed cabbage roses print chintz chair in God's waiting room, away from the loud, insane drumbeat of war, pain, and death. I'd like to take a long winter's nap. (For years I've dreamed of going to heaven for fifteen minutes and sitting on God's lap for a while. That's never worked out, so now I just think about a soft cushy chair in God's waiting room.) Or maybe I could take a sabbatical leave for a year or two. Doesn't that sound nice? I think it would be fun to do nothing more taxing than twiddling my thumbs and breathing normally. I have never thought of breathing normally as being fun, but that tells you how long it's been since I've done it. Sounds great to me.

If resting sounds great to you too, then I'm going to venture a guess here. You and I are probably sitting fairly close to each other in the same waiting room.

We've heard the diagnosis of our illness; we know

what's wrong with us. We understand the severity and nature of our pain, and we have chosen to change our attitudes concerning all this. But down in the most intimate part of our souls, we're tired. Life has hammered us unmercifully, and we've been battered by far too many blows. Although our spirits argue that we must "take action" and are even willing to do so, our minds and our emotions are so tired we just can't seem to get with the program. We want to lie down and rest. The last thing we want to do is "get up there and do something." We don't believe we've any strength or energy left.

We don't want to talk about going anywhere or doing anything. Some of us don't even want to talk about recovery. We're exhausted. Why can't we just sit this dance out? We've survived, so why do we have to "do something" to recover? Then, there are those scary questions like, how do we know what will happen next? Will we go into bankruptcy or get breast cancer? Where will the next blow come from? Will this ever end?

My dear person sitting next to me in God's waiting room, when we do not get up and move on, when we do not take initiative, when we are so tired that we do not think the risk of taking action is worth the effort, I promise you, we will suffer infinitely more pain than we already have. We will go sour, as they say in medical circles when a patient's vital signs begin to deteriorate after surgery. And frankly, life is too short to live the rest of our lives in sourness. I've seen too many broken people afraid or unwilling to choose to take action so that the sweet wholesome fragrance of God has lifted from their lives and a rancid and repulsive stench has remained.

I don't want that to happen to me. I don't want to grow old and embittered, and I suspect you really don't want that either. I also don't want to sit forever idle in God's waiting room waiting for something, anything, *whatever* to happen. I can't keep on sitting here hoping that I'll win the Pulitzer prize or the Nobel prize and that you'll win the ten-million-dollar lottery as we wait.

The truth is that even though this *is* God's waiting room and we are his children . . . life has not stopped nor have we taken an unexpected leave of absence from it. We were created for this life which is going on full blast all around us. Once in a while life stands fairly still and, for a moment or two, is mercifully quiet. But more often than not, life rolls, heaves, shifts, moves, and registers a 7.3 on the Richter scale.

So it seems to me that if you and I are ever going to progress from sour brokenness to sweet wholeness, we will have to lovingly and fully embrace the fact that:

Recovery requires firm decisions of our will, demanding that we change or alter our "last freedom" to choose our attitude.

Recovery comes with our willingness to honestly deal with the sufferings of our lives.

Recovery insists that we take the initiative which lies in all of us, and do something.

Recovery presses home the reality that when we get up, even though it feels as if both our legs are shattered beyond repair, we can begin to take steps toward healing.

I don't remember what I said at that conference after Francis told me to "get up there and . . . do something." But I am learning daily what it takes to get up and do something about recovery from the wounding of the past and about the preparation of my heart for the wounding of the future.

I am in the process of recovery. I shall probably never have a "full recovery" until my brief, albeit painful, journey ends at heaven's gates. But let me tell you about some recovery actions I have found to work in my life as I have used the option of choosing my attitudes.

First, I must be willing to trust God to help me forgive.

It seems just about every time anyone wants to advise me on how to recover, or someone comes up with the reasons for every pain I've ever had, they manage to lay an incredible guilt trip on my soul about *my* need to forgive. Usually, they act as if all of my hurts would go away in an instant if I'd humble myself, if I'd stop being so stubborn and selfish and just forgive.

It's perfectly reasonable that so much attention should be paid to our need to be forgiven and our need to forgive others, for forgiveness is another one of the great and basic tenets of our faith. The Bible presents the urgent truth of forgiveness as to its necessity, its healing power, and its ability to bring us a lasting joy.

But I guess I've always been fascinated by a number of sermons, books, and people who write or talk on forgiving others. They seem to dwell on two attack fronts. First, they are very clear in pointing out that I should forgive others (as if I didn't already know that), and second, they make my forgiving others sound like such a terribly simple matter. They imply that forgiving someone is as easy as snapping my fingers or waking up one morning and deciding, "Okay. I'll forgive so and so" and then the whole issue is over, forgotten, and resolved. Give me a break. We all know that few things in life are ever as simple as that. (This kind of thinking rates right up there with telling a hurting human being that the reason he isn't recovering from cancer, a loved one's death, or a divorce is because there is sin in his life or he doesn't have enough faith. Both things may be true or false in his life, but how would any of us know? Nowhere in the scriptures does God ever relinquish his job as the all-knowing yet merciful judge.) And rarely do I hear or read about these same "experts" applying the same truth about forgiving others in their own lives.

So how do I find the path to take me to the place of forgiveness in my mind and heart? What are the real issues?

Certainly, they are not my own petty frustrations over people who lay guilt trips on me regarding my agenda in the forgiveness arena. But I have to wonder . . . when one of these experts does insist that I forgive others, why am I so easily hurt, so quickly defensive, and so readily hostile? Why is my coming to this place of forgiveness so complicated and so laborious? And worse, why is it so easy for me to forgive and give grace to some people while forgiving and giving grace to others is as threatening as a trip to the dentist's office to have a root canal?

As I've looked at forgiveness (or rather my resistance to it) in my own life, I believe part of the answer lies in the fact that when it comes to forgiving someone I really love or care about, my inner want-to is strong and healthy, so I just do it. I take the initiative. But when it comes to forgiving someone, a friend or a stranger, who has verbally peeled and skinned me alive, I find myself at the corner of Can't and Won't streets. I can't forgive because I won't forgive.

Our pastor friend, John Hagee, said in a sermon not

too long ago, "The one you can't (or won't) forgive controls your life."

Now, there's no way I'm going to sit still, proudly proclaiming that because of what he or she did to me I'll never forgive them, not on your life or mine, especially if John is right (and I'm quite sure he is). I don't want anyone, particularly someone who has hurt me, controlling my life, for pity's sake!

Look at this lineup of hurdles I'm going to have to jump over in order to deal with forgiving those who have really wounded me. If I do forgive them:

1. I'll have to give up my right to strike back. (Ouch.) It's biblical, but giving up my urge to hit back doesn't seem to be one of my natural gifts.

2. They may get away with what they did or said. In fact, they may never be punished for the havoc they've brought about. (Oh no.)

3. It may appear to others that I've "given in"; therefore, it makes me look guilty or wrong about some issue and lets them walk away smelling like a rose and totally blameless. (I can't believe it.)

4. It also may appear to others that they have won! They may even be smug about it and brag how they've won and gotten the best of me.

5. Worse, they may pack up the whole problem in a storage box somewhere and just go on with their lives, never dealing with the issues of our need for resolution. (That leads nowhere.)

6. But here's the biggie. Let's say I do forgive them and that causes me to begin to feel good toward them. Whoops. Frankly my dear, that doesn't feel good, even a little bit. I don't want to like them; they've stabbed me

too many times, and they haven't spoken to Francis or
me for six years! (How true.)

Yes, John, you are so right! When I don't forgive those
people who have wounded me, they *do* control me—my
fears, my self-worth, my sense of justice, and even my lens
for seeing right and wrong.

Sometimes my problem with forgiving others is that
I'm more concerned with how my forgiveness might be
abused by others than with how God can use it as medicine for my healing. In "looking out for myself," I am
actually preventing my own recovery. If I really want to
look out for myself, I must begin really, seriously to trust
God to help me do something that is very difficult for me
to do on my own; that is, look beyond my own defensive-
ness and do what is right, regardless of how it feels and
in spite of the risk that someone may take advantage of
me or get the best of me.

We should "look out for ourselves" by taking care of
our physical, emotional, and spiritual health. And we
need to see that forgiving others is one of the major keys
to our own well–being. In their heart-healing book on
symptoms, cures, and causes of depression, *Happiness Is
a Choice* (Grand Rapids: Baker, 1978), Doctors Frank
Minirth and Paul Meier of the Minirth-Meier clinics recommended forgiving others, such as parents, counselors,
our mate, those in authority over us, and "others" who
have at some time wronged us, and releasing our bitter
anger toward God, as part of the healing process for depression.

I need to see to my physical nourishment, and I need
to do what is biblically and humanly right. The forgiveness process will never begin in my life until I consciously

decide that forgiving others is the right thing to do, no matter how it appears or feels to me.

This brings me back full circle to that word *trust.* Having clearly decided that being obedient in forgiving others is the right thing to do, here are some choices and actions that just may speed up recovery in an amazing way. The reason I can confidently write about these concepts is because they are presently working in my own life and healing is happening.

I need to ask God's help in leaping across the chasm from won't to will.

---

1. I need to be honest. I must frankly admit to myself and to the Lord that sometimes I don't want to forgive. It's not a matter of I can't; it's really I just won't. I need to ask for God's help in leaping across the chasm from won't to will. I cannot do this alone or by my own puny resolve. I must tap into the power of the Holy Spirit; otherwise, I'll fail. I'm too broken, in too much pain, and entirely too close to the whole mess to forgive someone or even to be objective. I need to be willing to trust God for his intervening help in forgiving the people I believe have inflicted or contributed pain in my life.

2. I need to forgive with my mind, even if I can't manage it right now with my feelings. I know that when I choose to obey God and choose an action that is the "right thing to do," my action may have to precede my feelings. That action, in the final analysis, determines the

attitudes and levels of my emotions. My feelings are important, but my mental behavior is so essential to action that forgiving in my mind is the first priority.

The woman who was pulled out of her Sunday school class as she was teaching the fifth graders because the church leaders had just found out she was divorced or the woman who was shunned from the church she's attended for years because her son was gay and died of AIDS is not going to be eager to forgive those who skinned her alive, all in the name of Christianity. Chances are that these and countless others of us are not going to have warm fuzzy feelings toward anyone who has sorely hurt us. So we need to trust God first, mentally, and obey him, knowing that later on our emotions will catch up to our obedience and our feelings will be more healed.

3. I must choose actions that show forgiveness. Perhaps I can write a letter, do tiny but kind deeds, or speak a gentle word. But more than that, I must refuse to do or say anything that demonstrates lingering resentments and unresolved forgiveness. I need to check out what I say about him or her to others, and if I find myself bad-mouthing those people to others, it's a pretty sure thing that I've gone back to "I *won't* forgive them." Please don't misunderstand me here.

I am not, repeat *not*, saying I can forgive and forget. Some hurts are so heinous that we (with God's help) will be able to bring about forgiveness, but because we are humans we are not able to forget the incidents, the cruel words or the destructive blows. Our memories will remain. I know from personal experience that memories and remembered pain can be healed, but I don't think they'll be completely erased out of our emotions until we

are on the other side of heaven's gates. This reality, however, should not keep us from finding ways to show our
forgiveness.

I wish that I had the money to send huge gorgeous
flower arrangements to about fifteen or twenty people
who dropped our friendship or our working relationship
six years ago. If I could, the message on the card would
read, "I'm grateful for all the bouquets you sent me in
the past. Enjoy this one and may God continue to bless
you."

However, I'm sure the florist's bill would equal the
national debt, so both Francis and I have found and used
other ways to call and show our forgiveness to these people. Some folks have responded; others haven't, but not
to worry. It feels wonderful to be able to show forgiveness
in the midst of remembered pain and present recovery.

4. Now this is an equally hard task but I need again to
be honest with God and myself about the reality that if I
have wronged someone, I need to ask his or her forgiveness with no strings attached.

I remember the day I asked my dad's forgiveness fully
expecting him to respond with, "Joyce, please forgive me
too," but an apology never came. I must seek forgiveness
where I have caused the problem; forgiving others
whether or not they forgive me. Years later, I truly believe
that our wonderful relationship during the last two years
of my dad's life was because of this principle of asking
forgiveness of a person without expecting any apology in
return. The day I apologized to him a few years before
his death may have been the determining factor in both
our recoveries.

5. I need to recognize that if my hurt from some individual is so deep seated that my unforgiveness persists

(thereby allowing that person to exercise enormous power and control over my mind and emotions), I may need to seek help through professional counseling. I must not be too proud to ask someone for help, nor should I be so naively self-centered as to think that I can handle this on my own.

Not too long ago, I received some shocking and hideous information about a man I know. The thought of forgiving him was as repulsive and out of the question as my petting a rattlesnake. But at God's nudging, my husband, Francis, put in a call for me to our trusted counselor, Dr. Pannabecker. I probably would have never been able to forgive the individual without the help of Dr. Pannabecker. From him, I received the insight and strength I needed to carry through with the action of forgiving the very person who had so grievously wounded me. The doctor gave me some much-needed understanding of that other person by his expert explanations and restored my sense of sanity in the midst of insanity. But I needed to hear his words and accept his help; otherwise, this godly psychologist's great counsel would have been lost somewhere in the phone connection.

If you are standing at the place of being unable to quell the dark spirit of unforgiveness about the person who has wounded you to the point of death, I pray God gives you a Dr. Pannabecker or a Minirth-Meier Clinic (the best) or one person you trust more than anyone in the whole world to talk to. Seek help. For there are some things that, because we are too close to the pain, we can only feel, not think. And if we keep this to ourselves, the healing of forgiveness is prevented from happening, thereby thwarting our recovery. When you find help, accept it and run with it.

Secondly: After I trust God to help me forgive, I must ask God to help me trust people again.

It takes only a few individuals who break our confidences and shatter our trust or just a loved one here or there who misunderstands or misjudges our words or actions or a couple of friends who silently steal away, remain quiet and disappear out of our lives to make us terribly reluctant, even allergic to trusting others again.

I admit, I've been learning to trust people again at a pitifully slow pace. Soon after my marriage to Francis I was interviewed on a Christian radio show. The host asked me to talk of some of the things I'd learned during the heartache of the past few years and also asked if there was something I would do differently now if I could.

I opened my mouth before I put my mind in gear and gave the interviewer a little more of Joyce than he bargained for. Faster than a good knee-jerk reaction or a speeding bullet, I blurted, "I wish I had not trusted my brothers and sisters in Christ so completely," adding that if I had the past year to live over that I'd never trust Christians again. "No, siree," I said, digging the verbal hole I was in a little deeper, "I'd never do that again." The young man's eyes widened in surprise, and I was immediately horrified and embarrassed that I had been so outspoken.

Later, as I pondered that outburst of mine, I saw that though I was feeling betrayed and abandoned by those men and women in the body of Christ, the right thing to do was definitely the opposite of pulling away from them. I realized I desperately needed to ask the Lord to help me trust people again. We need each other. We need each other no matter how some people fail or disappoint us or even turn against us and hurt us. We need to risk trusting each other. I am finding that trusting people again is a very large factor in recovery, especially in mine.

There's a precious story in Second Corinthians. Paul was writing and telling the people in the city of Corinth that when he and his band of co-workers arrived in Macedonia they were feeling nothing but dread and fear. The next line he wrote is this: "Then God who cheers those who are discouraged refreshed us by the arrival of Titus" (2 Cor. 7:6 LB).

I guess everyone, Paul, the people of Corinth, you and I all need a balcony person like Titus. It's okay if it is only one person. We need that one person, at least, whom we can trust to be our friend.

I've been blessed by the Tituses in my life like my husband, Francis, who is loving, sensitive, and best of all, accepting of me. Other members of my family and a few dear friends have become Tituses to me as well. I couldn't exist without their love and care. But I understand anyone's reluctance in risking friendship with others or the vulnerability of taking action to build bridges to strengthen relationships. I know how natural it is to feel wary of other people's motives or hidden agendas. We all wonder which side of the coin we will see. Will we be hurt again or will we find ourselves in a balcony support group, surrounded by Tituses?

For the sake of my recovery, however, I have to set aside my fears and just trust. Trusting is essential for me to reach out and establish relationships between myself and others. I need to construct those bridges of comfort, love, and aid to others. I need God's help in learning to trust again, but still, it is up to me to take the proverbial bull by the horns. I need to make the moves; I need to do something and forge into life new balcony relationships based on trust. I need to do that even if I am still anxious about how others have responded in the past or will respond now.

If we are ever to come to terms with our lonely "disconnectedness," then we will have to do something to "connect" with others. Despite the abuse each of us has felt or suffered at the hands of other people, we must refuse to let that cripple us from moving into new, loving, and trusting relationships.

It is no wonder that Jesus made trusting others and loving and caring for one another such an incredibly big deal—a commandment yet! He knew that in our lifetime our feelings of emotional pain, rejection, and abandonment would, at times, threaten to drown us in a raging flood of serious distrust. So seeking God's help in trusting and loving one another for the bonding of our hearts and minds with one another is a God-idea. It's as vital and necessary to an abundant life, a life of not merely existing, as eating, sleeping, and making love.

My son, Rick, and I were talking about a phrase a wise and gifted friend of his and Teresa's had used. The man had told them to "dispel the disbelief." I wrote the words down and asked Rick what "dispel the disbelief" meant to him.

He explained that when he was having a conversation with someone who said or communicated something to him that he didn't understand or he didn't like or maybe he didn't want to hear, he almost automatically began to believe the worst about the person and what he was hearing. So it was then that he would tell his mind to *dispel the disbelief* about this person and stop jumping to the wrong conclusions. Rick waited a moment while that was sinking into my brain and then flashed his most handsome smile and suggested that since it really seemed to work for him maybe I ought to try it out if or when it was needed. (Smart aleck kid.)

But he was right.

I need to choose to trust people again. I need to reach out and build intimate relationships with a few balcony people. I need to expect to find more Tituses. And when as the few people whom I do love are talking to me and I suddenly feel the clammy hand of distrust and surprise moving across my soul, I must dispel the disbelief so that with childlike wonder I can see and enjoy that loving relationship which contributes such comfort and pleasure to my life and thereby to my recovery progress.

I can tell you from recent incidents that asking God to help me trust others again not only is working but feels wonderful. But it is a decision of my will. I choose to trust. It is my choice.

Thirdly: After I trust God to help me forgive and then ask God to help me trust people again, I must trust God to help me feel and be useful.

I admit that I've not given a whole lot of thought to how much my recovery is dependent on taking care of my need to be needed by others and to feel useful. But birthdays (I've just had one) have a way of bringing hidden fears and other emotions that go bump in the night sharply into focus. And ranking right up there with a few other scary notions is the lingering fear that the older I grow the less I will be needed by my loved ones. I am afraid I will feel as if I am useful to no one, God included. I call it the "discarded syndrome."

There's nothing like waking up in the morning with a gut-wrenching feeling which announces to my brain that I've outlived my purpose and my reason for being here. It whispers that I'm certainly no longer needed or wanted by my family, friends or associates. Those kinds of early morning thoughts send the loud and clear message that I can be crumpled up like a piece of scrap paper and tossed out, discarded. It is indeed scary to believe even briefly that one is out of a job in this lifetime because one is not needed or useful anymore.

I remember the numerous times my Aunt Grace yelled and pleaded with my grandmother. She yelled because Grandma was stone deaf, even with both her hearing aids on, and pleaded because Grandma was in her late seventies. Aunt Grace always repeated the same requests. "Ma," she'd yell, "Ma, you listen to me! You've gotta take it easy now. You don't have to work anymore. We'll take care of you. . . . Ma, why are you putting on your coat? You don't have to walk to the corner grocery store or buy anything. I'll take care of shopping. I'll drive you." On and on my Aunt Grace would go, but Grandma just stubbornly shook her head, and each day she put on her coat, plopped her little black hat on the top of her silver hair, grabbed her mesh shopping bag, and walked to the store . . . just as she had done for more than fifty years. Finally, Aunt Grace threw up her hands and said, "Oh just let her go to the store!"

I believe Aunt Grace came to that realization because she understood that going to the store was Grandma's way of pulling her own weight, of feeling like she was doing her share of the work for the good of the family. Letting her go was an action of love which made Grandma feel she was needed and useful and an integral part of our lives. Even when Grandma was in her eighties, with her fingers knotted and gnarled by arthritis, and in much pain, she had a need to be useful. She was especially thrilled if, when we visited, she could cook and serve some mouth-watering food she knew we'd love. For my uncle Pete, it was breaded pork chops. For my mother and me, it was those thin, delicious Hungarian pancakes (palacsinta). Grandma would hover over us as we ate, taking such pride in forcing us to have another pancake with powdered sugar and cinnamon, long after we were stuffed beyond satiation.

Grandma didn't want to be treated as if everyone could get along quite well without her, thank-you-very-much, as if she wasn't needed. It was no secret that she wasn't ready or willing to be all washed up, nor was she about to give in to the feeling of being all used up, a useless old lady, ready to be discarded on the trash heap and forgotten.

I saw this same need to be useful in Katie, my wonderful say-past-age-sixty cleaning woman, especially on the day I asked her if she had given any thought to retiring. She shot a look back at me which suggested I had a serious loss of sanity and declared, "No, ma'am, I'se ain't ever gonna quit. I'se worked all my life . . . so's my sistas. What's I gonna do at home, sit and look out da winda?"

This need to feel useful is not only in people at the far end of their lives. I've seen it in the very young. My seven-year-old granddaughter, Jennifer, thinks she's died and gone to heaven if she can "help" with making dinner, baking cookies, cleaning off the table after dinner or any other "real job," as she puts it, with her mother or father. When the "job" is finished she feels wonderful about herself and her contribution. She feels like a team member . . . a vital part of her family.

I've come to think over the years that our need to be useful is no accidental or fleeting feeling that comes and goes within us. It is, rather, an inherent, deep-rooted desire that God himself has permanently placed in our emotions. The moment we sense we are being needed by and useful to others, the feeling brings an immense measure of personal satisfaction and a glowing, reassuring feeling that our mission is being accomplished and that there is purpose in our being alive.

When my babies were born, they were unable to care for themselves. Babies, as you've probably noticed, are completely helpless and totally dependent on others. My babies were no different. They needed me with all their little mights! And as I fed them, bathed and clothed them, loved and comforted them, I felt not only the bonding process melding us together, but I felt fulfilled by a sense of purpose. What love and care I gave away to them, I got back a thousandfold.

My grandmother, Katie my cleaning lady, precious Jennifer, and I have all felt the same thing. As we have carried out acts of usefulness to others, we have been rewarded for our efforts with that fulfilling fragrance found in the satisfaction of having been needed and having done something worthwhile. And strangely, as we have reached out to others, we (and all of us) have found our own self-worth greatly enhanced.

I find it interesting that nobody is useful or feels a sense of purpose and personal esteem by themselves in isolation. Our usefulness has to be found in interacting with others and in making contact with others. So, as much as we have a need to be useful, that need can only be fulfilled by sharing with one another.

As I said a few pages back, I just celebrated (I use the word "celebrated" loosely) a birthday. Between phone calls from my children, grandchildren, a few close friends and Francis' singing a fun rendition of "Happy Birthday" (he changed the words considerably), I took a few moments to study the last birthday card my mother sent me in 1966, the year she died. The back of the card begins, "My dearest, My every prayer and wish in a daughter has been met." Then she wished me four things: spirited success, health, joy, and peace.

Her last words on the bottom of the card are a beautiful benediction to me as real in 1991 as it was in 1966. She wrote of God when she said, "May he bless abundantly in '66 and put you in a large place."

I smiled over her phrase about God putting me in a "large place," and then, as I occasionally do, I talked to her about the large place I'm in right now and how really, darling Mother, it doesn't feel very large at all.

But what do I know? Maybe I wouldn't recognize a large place if it was a deep well and I fell into it. And then again, maybe a large place is a little like a deep well . . . mmhmm? At any rate, I was cut short in my mental process by the realization that coupled with my intrinsic need to be useful is *God's* plan to put me in a "large place."

The thought then occurred to me that just perhaps I needed to take a much closer look at what I thought and believed about "large places."

Instantly, my definition of someone in a large place was a mental picture of Dr. Billy Graham's large place. God has put him in a large place which covers the whole world or the White House where he spent the night during the Persian Gulf crisis with President and Mrs. Bush. The large place for Mother Teresa is her unique religious order, the Society of the Missionaries of Charity, in Calcutta, India, practiced and known all over the world. But is that what "May God put you in a large place" really means?

No, I think that whether we are a world-famous person or a homeless, nameless individual the large place of our life is *anywhere* God has chosen to put us this very moment.

For instance, six years ago I thought I was in a very large place, much larger than I'm in now. After all, one could not pick up a Christian magazine without seeing my picture on the cover or reading an interview or article or finding a publisher's advertisement about my products. For years my books were on the National Religious best–seller list, often number one, and sometimes three books at a time. There were roughly seven million books and recordings by Joyce Landorf in circulation.

So it looked to me, and must have looked to others, like God had answered my mother's prayers in triplicate. Her daughter was indeed in a large place. It also appeared to everyone, including me, that I had turned out to be a highly useful person, that I was needed on this earth and that somewhere in the mix of things I was really being used of God.

In my thinking the large place meant being wanted, sought after, and courted and being "wined and dined" by pastors and publishers, being friends with best-selling authors, and knowing and hobnobbing with very famous Christians. I know now it can mean all those things for it is God who puts his children in large places. But I also know that a large place may be a completely different territory from what I initially thought.

During and after my divorce, I was removed from that large place which was so familiar to me. The royalties, the speaking engagements, the people seeking interviews, the publishers, the bouquets of flowers that filled my home on my birthday and the beautiful gifts given on Christmas all vanished. They were all whisked away, as it were, overnight.

All I could ask myself was what happened to the large place? But of greater concern to me was what happened to my being useful both to God and to others?

Many critical and judgmental voices clamored and shouted out at me then and some even do that now. Their loud voices told me that nobody wanted me anymore. They yelled that nobody was reading my books or listening to my tapes, that the only place my books could be found was on close-out tables of Christian bookstores and in garage sales. Those angry, sometimes cruel, voices pounded home their message to my heart. I was no longer useful to God and his kingdom so why didn't I get out of Christian work and go secular?

For a few years, it was impossible to ignore or turn off those voices as they continued their barrage of stony-hearted words. I began to believe that quite possibly they were right. I thought I'd never be asked to write, to speak or to sing again. I felt unwanted, unneeded, and unuseful, and believed that being in a *large place* was a thing of the past for me.

But I was wrong about large places.

I know now that a large place is not measured by size, success or world recognition, but by God's design. Who's to say that the nameless woman who touched the hem of

Jesus' garment was not in a very large place? Or that Mary, who gave birth to Jesus in a stable, was not in the largest place of her life? God's design, not ours, defines the measurements of large places in our lives.

. . . the place I'm in right now is the largest place of my life.

I know now that it is God who calls us to our mission and it is he who gave us the desire to be useful and it is he who decides exactly which large place he'll put us in. How foolish of me or anyone to think that God would somehow take back his calling, drain away all the desire he put into us to be useful, and then never use us. God doesn't do that. He just changes the field and the location, but it still is a *large place.* It can even be bigger than ever or smaller than ever, no matter what some people think or say.

Because of God's design, the place I'm in right now is the largest place of my life. I'm fifty-nine years old and my picture may never again dominate the Christian magazines. Publishers and royalties may never be what they once were. Scores of people may not scramble over one another to be attentive or in order to obtain my services for their church, publishing company, television, or radio show. But none of that really matters as long as I know that the God we serve has equipped all of us to be useful and it is he who puts us in large places.

As I was taking a really long look at the place I'm in right now, I was struck by the thought that it's highly possible that the place we are standing on right now, at this moment, is not only a wondrously large place but is every bit as holy as the ground beneath Moses' feet when he was communicating with God up there on the mountain. Think of it! Wherever we are this moment, God has put us here.

Our large place may appear to us as a very wide field, white with harvest, or as an obscure, narrow shelf. Who's to say that while some people may think we should be discarded as we've outlived our usefulness here on this earth, God has, in fact, put us according to his plan in the very best, the greatest, the largest place of our lives. *Active* or *shelved*, it is still a large place because God has placed us there.

I have come to the point in my prayer life that even if the large place I'm in covers only a very small territory . . . it's still holy ground. If my large place is never again to go worldwide or do so and so and such and such . . . then, that's just fine. So be it. Or if I'm not to reach some breathtaking pinnacle of success, achieve this or that, receive this big award or gain status among my peers again, that's fine. So be it.

What's of paramount importance here is that you and I have been put by God right now in this large place and we can trust him with our inborn need and desire to be useful. *Where* we serve does not matter, and *what* others think of our sphere of service and usefulness does not matter either. It only matters that we continue to serve him, that we continue to share Christ's love and forgiveness with others, that we continue to turn our brokenness and pain into gifts of hope for others around us who are shattered. And when we doubt or wonder whether God is in our serving, we need to remember the apostle

Peter's words, "God has given each of you some special abilities; be sure to use them to help each other, passing on to others God's many kinds of blessings" (1 Pet. 4:10 LB).

What is important now is that the large place we are in today is the very place we've been searching for all our lives. Because this place, this holy ground we are standing on, gives us the chance to choose to have an attitude pleasing to God and healing to mankind. Here we are, in this incredibly large place, presented with countless golden opportunities to serve God and others and to be extraordinarily useful.

My mother's birthday card of twenty-five years ago was quite prophetic after all: God has very definitely put me in a large place. In my mind's eye, I can see her up there looking past the incredible beauty of heaven through the skies toward earth. She's just found out from some heavenly source that things with her daughter don't appear to be going so well. She sees that yet another earthly tragedy has struck a telling blow. She sees that her Joyce-Honey is suffering pain from a new affliction. But as I see her in my mind's eye, Mother doesn't seem to be too greatly upset about what she sees. In fact, the expression on her face can only be described as serene and pleased. Quite pleased.

I see her turn to my father, who is beside her peering down over heaven's balustrade, and I can hear the lilt in Mother's voice as she says to him, "Oh, look Clifford, isn't that just wonderful of God. He's just put our Joyce-Honey in another large place!"

Yes! Yes! Yes!

I choose to trust my loving sovereign God no matter what I face or where I'm put. And guess what, not only will I survive but I shall recover, and I'll recover in the grandest manner possible. So will you if you catch the vision about the "large place" you're in right now.

Peter was writing about pain (present and future) and of our choice to trust God, when he wrote, "So if you are suffering according to God's will, keep on doing what is right and trust yourself to the God who made you, for he will never fail you" (1 Pet. 4:19 LB).

What a promise! What a comfort! To me this is a real keeper. The choice is mine, the choice is yours. The only freedom which can never be drained, whipped, or beaten out of us is the freedom to choose our attitudes.

We can choose to trust ourselves to the God who made us, who created us for this time, and who put us into this large place . . . for he never, never fails us.

Here, take my hand, let's trust God together for our survival and for our recovery. Then let's by faith believe that our recovery is taking place now, this very moment.

NOTES

Chapter 1

1. Desmond, "A Pencil in the Hand of God," *Time*, Dec. 4, 1989.
2. Dr. Robert A. Cook, *Always Something Better*, prepared for publication by Mildred M. Cook for Kings College, Briarcliff Manor, New York, 10, 12.
3. Viktor Frankl, *Man's Search for Meaning* (Boston, MA: Beacon Press, 1959), 86. Reprinted by permission.
4. *Ibid.*, 86.
5. *Ibid.*, 86–87.
6. *Ibid.*

Chapter 2

1. Charles Schulz, *Peanuts, Medical Economics,* April 4, 1990.
2. Susan Howatch, *Glittering Images* (New York: Ballantine, 1988), 70. From GLITTERING IMAGES by Susan Howatch. Copyright © 1987 by Leaftree Limited. Reprinted by permission of Alfred A. Knopf Inc.
3. J. B. Phillips, *Good News* (New York: MacMillan, 1963), 1.
4. *Ibid.*, 2.
5. *Ibid.*, 3.
6. *Ibid.*, 6.
7. *Ibid.*, 7.
8. George MacDonald, *The Gentlewoman's Choice*, ed. by Michael R. Phillips (Minneapolis, MN: Bethany, 1987), 110. Reprinted by permission of Bethany Publishing House.

Chapter 3

1. Sheldon Vanauken, *A Severe Mercy* (San Francisco: Harper & Row, 1977).
2. "Healin' Stream," © 1989 by KRISTOSHUA MUSIC (BMI). Administered by CMI, Nashville, TN. All rights

reserved. International copyright secured. Used by special permission.
3. Charles Reynolds Brown.
4. Amy Carmichael, *Candles in the Dark* (Christian Literature Crusade, 1988), 15.

Chapter 4

1. Sam Shoemaker, *Extraordinary Living for Ordinary Men* (Grand Rapids, MI: Zondervan, 1965), 8.
2. Keith Miller, "Short Cut Home" reprinted with permission of Keith Miller, Copyright © 1984.

Chapter 5

1. Henri Nouwen, *The Wounded Healer* (New York: Image/ Doubleday, 1979), xvi.
2. Lyrics by Claire Cloninger. Music by Jeff Kennedy. " 'Til You Hear the Music," Word, Inc. Reprinted by permission of C. A. Music/ASCAP, Copyright © 1984, All Rights Reserved, International Copyright Secured.
3. Robert Louis Stevenson, *Travels In Hawaii* (Honolulu: Univ. of Hawaii Press, 1973).
4. Quoting from the writings of Father Damien Joseph de Veustec, 1885.
5. Nouwen, *The Wounded Healer,* 93.
6. *Ibid.,* 100.

Chapter 6

1. The Reverend Arthur Brooks, D.D., in *Perennials* by Rt. Rev. Phillips Brooks, D.D. (New York: E. P. Dutton, Copyrighted 1898, Published 1909), 160.
2. Rt. Rev. Phillips Brooks, D.D., *Perennials* (New York: E. P. Dutton, Copyrighted 1898, Published 1909), 74.
3. *Ibid.,* 75.
4. *Ibid.,* 48.
5. *Ibid.,* 56.
6. *Ibid.,* 67.
7. *Ibid.,* 77.
8. *Ibid.,* 79.
9. *Ibid.,* 88.
10. *Ibid.,* 107.
11. *Ibid.,* 152.
12. *Ibid.,* 152.

13. Martha Snell Nicholson, "The Thorn," in *The Glory Forever* (Chicago: Moody, 1951), 31.
14. Amy Carmichael, *Candles in the Dark* (Fort Washington, PA: Christian Literature Crusade/Dohnavur Fellowship, 1982), 73.
15. Shoemaker, *Extraordinary Living,* 37.